i

Printed in the United States of America

First Printing, 2019

ISBN 978-0-578-60408-4

Angel Wisdom, LLC
2300 New Road
Suite 201C
Northfield, NJ 08225

www.ColleenStMichaels.com

Heightened & Enlightened
Publishing Company

Credits
Cover Graphics- Ray Nuzzi Photography, LLC
Editor and Ghostwriter: Danielle Ingraham
Heightened & Enlightened Publishing Co.- Colleen St. Michaels

THE OTHER SIDE OF ADDICTION

The Afterlife

Colleen St. Michaels

Dedication

Thank you, Gianna and Cole! I love you, my beautiful children. Thank you for trusting in me each step of our adventure together. Many times we were going into the unknown, but our love for one another and faith always kept us safe.

To my ground angel: thank you for being my lover, best friend, and my number one fan. You saw in me, from day one, the pieces of me that I was still assembling. Your steady support and unwavering goodness have been a gift to me.

Thank you to my family for being who you are and for all your support.

To Danielle: my assistant, friend, editor, and ghostwriter. Thank you doesn't seem to suit. Your capacity to organize my business and allow me to do what I love every day is a blessing. I appreciate your amazing ability to interpret my channeled writing as I am speed writing so I don't miss a message.

Thank you to all of my clients that I have had the pleasure of sitting with. Your invitation for me to enter into your world intimately at a time of healing is an honor and privilege.

Table of Contents

Disclaimer:

This self help and interactive workbook was designed to assist easing the mind and offering suggestions to promote healing. Colleen is not a doctor, therapist, or any other type of health care professional. She is a Spiritual Medium who works with Angels and our Loved Ones passed.

Who Am I?

My name is Colleen and I am an Angel Intuitive and Spiritual Medium. The metaphysical world has many branches, each person having their own unique way of receiving information. I have intuitive abilities, but I do not receive future events or lottery numbers. My gift's focus is on delivering the information for healing and to guide people in developing their own unique connection with intuition. Each of us was born with this ability to connect with spirits and our loving team of angels. Here is some insight about my spiritual gifts, so you can better understand as we move through this book.

I am a Spiritual Empath. In the spiritual world, it is referred to as Clairsentience. It is the feeling of thoughts, feelings, and emotions of others. It is a heightened sensitivity to environments and the emotions of people.

I am also Claircognizant- meaning clear knowing or knowing without knowing why. I hear the information through my thoughts in varying tones. It is in my inner voice that I receive a message, but I know that this not information that I would know in everyday life. I can pick up on details and descriptions of places, people, or environments I have not had prior access to.

Clairvoyance is called spiritual sight- the ability to receive images or pictures in the physical world or in the mind. I see movies or flashes of information within my spiritual sight. I like to call this my spiritual theater.

If this is all new to you and seems different or weird, I completely understand! Something brought you to read this book and I ask that you take a breath, be open, and read on. I was raised Catholic and this was not in my upbringing to do anything other than pray to God. Nowhere in my high school senior yearbook did it say this would be my work, but I feel so grateful everyday this it is.

Even though I have always had a curiosity and love for all people, I understand now why I always felt drawn to people when they were hurting. I felt all they need is to be heard and understood. I am so grateful that I listened to the strong voice within and a gentle nudge to push past my fears and open Angel Wisdom years ago.

Author's Note

I will be the first to say, I am not an expert in addiction. My experience and expertise are surrounded in areas of healing. When I meet your loved one for the first time, I see them as beautiful souls; I see them as love.

When I meet your loved one, there is no suffering, pain, illness, or any manipulator holding them hostage from the life you wanted them to live. I see them as the truth and they speak to you in a soul loving truthful way.

My first intention for writing this book is based around what I have witnessed when I meet with families struggling with the darkness of this epidemic. It is emotionally paralyzing to families; not just affecting the one that struggles with addiction. It is the addiction after the addiction.

As a medium, I am on the front lines between peace and pain. They are at peace while you are in a stage of pain. Some people are staying in the dense space of their pain. I am here to show you that you do not have the live the rest of your life in pain. Your loved one does not want you to live in pain. The ones who were addicted are now in peace and they want you as their loved ones to be at peace as well.

After years of trying to save someone's life who was struggling to save their own, I find families coming in emotionally beaten up with thoughts and feelings of helplessness. I want families to find peace and happiness in their lives again.

My second intention for writing this book is to guide you with the information that I am given to share. I cannot change your experience prior to reading this- nothing anyone says or does can do this. However, I feel it is part of my responsibility to share the information that can help guide your healing.

There is another side to addiction and that is the families that are now left with their loss of their loved one. That other side is you. You are now in a club that you never volunteered to be in but has many members. You have lost a loved one to addiction and I feel for you.

This dreadful epidemic is robbing families of husbands, wives, children, and siblings. Advocates of addiction are doing amazing tasks to bring awareness globally to this epidemic. It saddens me to watch this epidemic take out families. Addiction is not only a personal disease, but a family disease. I know that your loved ones are safely on the other side, but what do we do for those left behind?

Introduction

My Dear Reader,

None of us are immune to experiencing loss. The feelings of pain and grief are most often associated with death. The epidemic of drug addiction in the United States has left countless numbers of individuals and families turned upside down. In my work as an angel intuitive and spiritual medium, I am witnessing firsthand the plague of pain. I can no longer stand on the sidelines and wait for people to come in for a session and come to me; I need to go to the people. It is not acceptable to watch the lives of everyone involved hurt. It is not acceptable to watch as the darkness in the world profits on pain.

I am often asked, "Why do you care so much? Who have you lost to addiction?" The answer is no one in my immediate surroundings has passed away from an overdose. However, it does not need it to be in my personal world to love and have compassion. This epidemic has proven that anyone, in any family, can face this reality at any time. I promote trying to connect families that are hurting and connect active addicts to resources that can offer assistance in finding them treatment facilities to help. I work with people living in recovery to guide them with the tools to self love and forgiveness.

The stigma that surrounds addiction needs to be lifted so that society becomes more educated and less punishing. It is only pushes people further into the dark with shame and embarrassment. A stereotype of who can be affected is an illusion. This beast does not discriminate by race, gender, religion or social status. This is everyone's epidemic- no one raises their hand and says this is the day I tear my world apart and everyone one I love. It is a slow drip that eventually becomes a flood.

I see addiction as a dark force that is a thief of the light and if I can offer light in your healing and lift dark moments so you have a moment of peace, only then am I fulfilling my purpose here. I see people living in the dense energy of grief and while this may seem grim, it is a privilege for me to be able to be a bridge between worlds and witness the subtle positive shifts in their perception.

Even though I may not know you personally, I would like to extend love and support to you. Whatever stage of grief you are experiencing right now, take from this book what you align with and leave the rest behind. As you progress on your healing journey, you may reference back to the book to have a different outlook of the information. As you will soon learn in later chapters, we are all connected in the afterlife; we are all created from the same source of light that we carry within our soul.

My words and intention are not about cheering you up or making you feel a momentary speck of peace. I fully acknowledge your pain and want nothing more than to support you. I do not want you to feel alone. Your pain is neither minimized nor dismissed in any part of this book.

I cannot change the experiences you have had leading up to you reading this book. But since you have lost a loved one to addiction, this is your truth and I am here to support you in the healing process. It is part of my life's purpose and passion on this earth to teach you about the world that most do not have access to. As an Angel Intuitive and Spiritual Medium who has been practicing for years, connecting thousands of families and their loved ones that are seeking answers to the myriad of questions that flood their mind each day is important. They are seeking peace and reassurance that their loved one is safely on the other side.

Join me as we journey to the world of the afterlife.

Love and Light,

Colleen St. Michaels

Chapter 1

Light is information. Darkness is lack of information.

When I connect with your loved one on the other side for the first time, I see them as *love*. There is no suffering, pain, or illness of any kind. The manipulator (addiction) is no longer holding them hostage from the life you wanted them to live. I see them at peace, healed, and all-knowing. They communicate with a deep understanding of the life they lived and their reality now. The communication is so beautiful; spoken in a soul-loving, truthful way.

We must first learn the background of how things work behind the scenes (the afterlife) so that when we move into the information that has been shared from your loved ones, the messaging makes sense. The steps to living and crossing over can be compared to a symphony. The series of instruments, when coming together, creates a harmony. Everything flows together methodically and in unison.

Light is information. Darkness is a lack of information.

This fundamental concept is important for everyone to acknowledge and live by. The soul is our purpose for being in this world. It is our belief system, the ability to forgive and show respect, our self-love, trust, faith, hope, and joy. The more informed we are, the more space we allow for the light to expand through us. As the light expands, it extinguishes the guilt, shame, despair, and helpless feelings that the dense energy of darkness had once occupied.

When speaking of darkness throughout this book, it correlates with low vibrational emotions- not evil. The absence of light can be our despair, fear, and hopelessness, our lack of values, self-love, or respect.

Think about it as if you were to walk into a dark room. Our vision is impaired and our sense of safety and trust are compromised. Without knowing your surroundings, you must find the door or light switch (both representing the light). When they cannot be found, it creates a sense of panic and fear in us. However, once we find the light or the door, we are filled with relief and joy. When we have a connection, it makes us feel secure.

When we have information, it leads to a greater support of understanding and healing. I encourage you to be open to the process of healing and willingness to absorb information. Healing, or grief, has many layers much like an onion; each layer must be peeled back with patience and compassion to reach the source of your discomfort. Between the passing of your loved one and living in the world of addiction, it has led you to reading this book.

Healing does not mean forgetting. Instead it gives us the opportunity to think about our loved one without associating them with heartache. Their addiction did not define their entire earthly existence. The beautiful memories that were made with you before their passing, is what you should cherish with your heart. This is not about remaining secluded in your sadness. You already have enough of that. It is about finding joy and purpose in life again.

I already know that you have experienced a rollercoaster of emotions through living this journey of addiction *sober*. In this book, I want to help show you how to strengthen the light already inside you and to then build and strengthen your personal communication and connection to your loved ones on the other side. We will go through the myths and truths that families will go through, hold on to, and create.

Trust in the love that you and your loved one shared on this earth is infinite. The connection to your loved one does not end when that person leaves this earth. The soul lives through you as you go through your day and watches over you by night. Love never dies or dissolves. It is endless. It is the only emotion that can coexist in both worlds. It can be challenging to accept that the spirit of the person can be around you rather than the physical person. I understand that if you had a blank canvas to paint on that you would paint a different picture. For the purposes of healing, you must have a realistic understanding of what is in front of you. The more healing we allow in, the greater the connection with the loved one that we seek. Throughout this book, you will be given the information and tools to redefine your new normal with the help of the invisible realm.

Notes _____

_____

_____

_____

_____

_____

_____

_____

_____

_____

_____

_____

_____

_____

_____

_____

_____

_____

_____

_____

Chapter 2

Soul Speak

Let's Go Soul Diving and Go in Deep

The existential question that always peaks our curiosity is, "Why are we here?" We are spirit beings doing a human experience. These next few chapters are going to support you in understanding the whole picture- life as we know it has a very different view from the afterlife.

All souls enter the world with all of the tools to navigate the journey through what we view as our Earth Walk. Love and intuition are the most important guidance systems embedded into the soul. Love on a soul level is created from an unconditional, unbreakable God-sourced energy. This love does not judge, harm, or leave us. Love on the human level is very conditional, based off of the nature of relationships, experiences, and perception. In this way, love on a human level can cause pain and suffering. On a soul level, however, love is infinite and pure, without pain or conditions. Part of our lesson here is to experience unconditional love for ourselves and others.

Once coming into the physical world at birth, we are gifted free will and free choice.

Free will is the opportunity for us to learn and grow to exercise the power of choice using our inner intuition. Otherwise, we would remain a soul and not need to take the journey into humanity. Every soul has an equal opportunity to grow and expand. We flourish during this life experience.

What Do You Feed Your Soul?

An old Cherokee man is teaching his grandson about life. "A fight is going on inside me," he said to the boy.
"It is a terrible fight and it is between two wolves. One is evil – he is anger, envy, sorrow, regret, greed, arrogance, self-pity, guilt, resentment, inferiority, lies, false pride, superiority, and ego." He continued, "The other is good – he is joy, peace, love, hope, serenity, humility, kindness, benevolence, empathy, generosity, truth, compassion, and faith. The same fight is going on inside you – and inside every other person, too."
The grandson thought about it for a minute and then asked his grandfather, "Which wolf will win?"
The old Cherokee simply replied, "The one you feed."
-Cherokee Proverb-

I love this proverb because it helps us to understand how unique each of our journeys are and how we have a say in to which side we feed. Even in the darkest moments, we have light. Even if it is a monetary flicker, we must acknowledge the power within us to expand this light and heal.

15

With free will, the only experiences in life we have control over are ones that we have created. There is an ownership and empowerment that comes with free will. We only have control over our own thoughts, feelings, and actions. That may be something you are familiar with in your mind, but when your heart gets involved it can be difficult to remember.

You cannot fail another human being.

The natural course of grief is frequently to blame yourself when the feelings of defeat set in. We must always remember we cannot fix situations or fail someone because it is their free will that needs to make decisions. It is not our responsibility to do so. Their free will has to exercise the right to make that decision.

You have done everything in your power to help your loved one to get better. I have met many who have gone as far as to drain all their financial resources in trying to help someone they love. You have stretched your boundaries to areas prior you did not know existed. You have negotiated with God and prayed for a different outcome. All of these acts of love were in the name of trying to save someone all while, ultimately, you had no control over their actions or choices.

The self-blame and mental warfare are keeping the pain alive within you as you reflect and revisit every painful thought. The mental battle is not offering you any peace in trying to cope with the loss of your loved one.

The willingness to shift your attention and connect deeply with the truth is how much you loved them. It is easy to love when everything is easy and in order; it is extraordinary to love when everything seems chaotic and out of control. Even though their outcome was your worst fear, you need to feel secure in the fact that you loved and you loved them hard. That is something you need to affirm and believe within yourself. We will discuss that in later chapters, but hold tightly to the words "love never dies".

Affirmations, when practiced daily, gently shift our perceptions. Here are sample affirmations to help cancel, clear, and delete the negative train of thought:

"I am worthy of healing."
"Love never dies."
"I loved unconditionally."
"I let go of this pain."
"It wasn't my fault."
"I choose peace."
"I did all I could."

Each soul comes into this world with a blueprint, or "soul chart". Prior to entering its human vessel, the soul has chosen lessons that will help it grow through human experiences and evolve on its journey on Earth. The soul craves the lessons for growth. It is the human perception that creates deception in how it is viewing the lessons as a positive or negative. If we do not grow or learn through a lesson, we will repeat a lesson over and over. These lessons are the pivotal point in one's growth, which is why it continues to be repeated.

Imagine having a manual that comes into the world with you at birth. In this manual, it has written the soul's birth date and end date and that determines the length of the manual. Some souls come for just a short stay and others for an extended visit. The pages that have our life lessons printed on them will be scattered throughout the manual. The blank pages around these lessons are where one creates their life's journey. At times when we see a loved ones struggling, we may abandon our book and jump on the pages where our loved one is stuck and struggling. You may help the person flip the page temporarily, but their soul has still not learned the lesson. Therefore, when you return to your own book, the page will turn back for other people until they themselves learn and work through their own lesson.

As an apparent and former enabler, I understand how easy it is to jump into another person's book. The angels often called me a *journey jumper*. I had trouble with the concept of allowing someone I loved to struggle and not try and fix it. I learned that each time that I would rescue or take over a situation that I did not create, that I was actually creating another opportunity for them to learn the lesson again and again.

A friend of mine who is a therapist explained to me that you can spend all your waking hours worrying and trying to find solutions, but it does not mean anything if the person you are worried about does not make the change. Change is a very personal commitment that takes great work in shifting the mental and physical belief for each individual. Many times we catch ourselves trying to pick up the broken pieces of another's life. It took me many hours studying with the angels, falling on my knees begging God to help me understand the value of allowing someone to live their journey and for me to live mine. It is possible and can be done with great love and respect for everyone involved. Each experience someone has is an opportunity for them to gain confidence and trust in their capability to do life. The most powerful lesson to build confidence is feeling capable.

Returning Home

The afterlife is home; the origin of where we come from. Whether you connect with God, a source, a creator, or the universe, this powerful light is within us; it is the soul's light. Different faiths have a variety of beliefs surrounding the afterlife. Having been raised Catholic, connecting with loved ones that have crossed and accepting it was foreign to me because it is not normally accepted in Catholicism. My views are not based on any one religion except my love of God and spirituality.

Each soul coming into the world is as unique as the human fingerprints of the hand that holds it. Our fingerprints match our soul prints in that they are individual to each of us. This is why we can never compare our journey to that of anyone else here on their earth walk. This is why we handle life and situations differently. If two people have the same experience then why does one person seem to have the ability to deal or move through the experience, whilst the other is left floundering and struggling? Personal perception is key to how we learn from separate events.

The soul comes here with full awareness that it has the tools and capabilities to overcome any obstacles that it has *chosen* to face during this human experience. The soul has all the coordinates to navigate through any experience bringing us to our highest potential. As a culture, we use chronological age as a standard of gauging where someone should be at different milestones in their life. Ways we see this with pertain to a legal drinking or voting age; how old we should be when we get married or have children; or how old people should be when it is acceptable to pass away.

With spirituality, we view the soul age as to how someone adjusts in life; we have young adults and old adults; souls may be young or old. Have you ever met a child who speaks with wisdom beyond their years? On the other hand, have you met the adult who does not want to grow up? A child in an adult suit, these souls often find themselves in the same situations, repeating lessons and behaviors over and over again. We all experience repetition, but the young soul may take longer to learn. The soul came here to learn lessons to grow and expand. We have this social construct where we think we should be at certain areas in our lives at certain time frames. Therefore, we may have difficulty understanding others' choices. The soul never judges any choices, ours or those of others. However, it is only in the human state in which we carry self-doubt, fear, worry, and judgment. This is all part of the Ego.

Now let us spiritually speak about the Ego. The Ego is not what gives us confidence to speak in front of a large crowd, but it is constant inner bully that harasses us from within our own minds. I refer to ego as the archive keeper of all the things that we do not want to remember and adds more to those stories, which in turn creates more pieces to your pain. The ego is the negative voice within, creating confusion and indecision. When speaking with loved ones on the other side, often they reference their ego and talk about how they could not quiet their thoughts and forgive themselves for hurting themselves and the people they love through their actions as an addict. When the soul returns home, it is entirely free of ego, suffering, confusion, illnesses, pain and judgment. Judgment is a human condition, not one of the divine.

In order to quiet our ego, I usually start by saying, "Ego out." This brings my higher self into focus and makes it easier to listen to my angels and those around me. If you still find your ego creeping in- and it will try- continue saying, "Ego out" until it goes quiets. The difference between our egos and the voices of those on a higher vibration is night and day. Like I said, our ego is the negative voice we hear. The voices of our angels and loved ones are always gentle and kind.

Why?

I often hear my clients asking why their prayers were not answered the way they wanted. They are left feeling as though God, or source figure, let them down. It is natural to send prayers and request for divine assistance when someone is struggling. No prayer ever goes unheard. Free will plays a huge role in this.

When you send a prayer requests on someone else's behalf, the divine immediately respond. Here is the catch: the person you are sending prayers to must release their free will to allow the healing in. The angels are always overseeing us as we journey through our earth walk, waiting for the release of free will to dive in and help. Angels have unconditional love for us and never want us to struggle or live in a way they were not intended to. Free will is released simply by saying help me and then being open to a different way. Often you, as the witness to addiction, feel helpless as you see a loved one struggling. When they do not allow help in, they are swimming in the density of self-punishment and the feelings of not being worthy of forgiveness. This is not their truth but their perception of themselves as good or bad.

The angels and divine never see us as *not enough* or see any act as unforgivable; but they see us as pure divine love. This is why it is important for you to focus on your healing and release yourself from being accountable for things that were out of your control. Calling on the angels to help support you as you grieve for comfort and love.

Notes _____

_____
_____
_____
_____
_____
_____
_____
_____
_____
_____
_____
_____
_____
_____
_____
_____
_____
_____
_____
_____

Chapter 3

Angels among us

Is my loved one now an angel?

I am asked each day if our loved ones who crossover become angels? The answer is no. We have two sets of divine assistants that are watching over us each moment here on our earth walk: one is our deceased loved ones who crossover and are now spirit/souls and the other is our team of adoring angels.

Well then, who are the angels? The angels are our divine cheerleaders and most devoted partners. They are non-denominational beings of light, created in pure divine source love. There are many levels of angelic assistance.

For the purposes of this book, we will focus on the archangels and guardian angels. Angels are governed by divine law, which states that they cannot interfere with the human free will. Angels have never walked the earth; they do not have the physical form of a human vessel or body. Often angels are pictured in texts showing large majestic wings that stretch far and wide. I see the angels as light, but have felt the embrace of the wings when I was sad, hurt, or frightened. Since angels are light beings, they are not gender specific, but they carry vibration of masculine and female energies. The energy type is determined by what type of assistance we are asking for.

The word angel derives from the Greek word *Angelos*, meaning "a messenger of God." We do not worship angels but partner with them to do the earth walk. When we send prayers up to God/source, angels eagerly move to our side. As we learned in the chapters before, free will must be released in order for a divine intervention to occur whether from our loved ones crossed or angels. The angels know our life purpose here and hold our life's blueprints. Angels see perfection when looking upon us, they have unconditional love and respect for us. Great respect is given when we enter this life. The angels know that we are going into a space where polarities exist and the power of choice to listen to our inner guidance or follow the voice of ego is present.

Our world is filled with temptation and opportunities to sway off of our original path. Angels do not judge us or punish us for moving off our destined path but offer us support and love to get back on the path we chose prior to coming into life. Since they do not have physical form, they can be available for any personal request at any time and the angels do not rank problems. We can never ask for too much assistance from the angels and no request is too large or too small. Nothing is more important than comforting and assisting you during any part of your day/night. The key to working with angels is to ask for help, express gratitude, and have patience. We cannot tell them how our request is to be played out.

We view our situations through a peephole in life, having attachments as to what and how things should turn out, whereas the angels have the blueprints and the panoramic view of our journey. The angels cannot do the work for us. As souls before entering this earth, we agreed upon soul lessons for growth. In knowing this, they can help guide us through our intuition and give us signs for direction. Each of us was born with the gift of intuition. It is up to each individual to listen and trust the inner guide that speaks intuitively through them. It is like a muscle when the muscle is exercised it expands and grows stronger, allowing you to trust it. The spiritual muscle works the same way. When we trust it, it becomes an amazing guide to living life.

The angels and our loved ones speak through our intuition to offer guidance. The information can be received through our physical body, our thoughts that seem to come out of nowhere, dreams, ringing of the ears, or through another human. For example, you may be in the middle of a conversation and the person you are conversing with says something that your ears catch; the piece of information that answers your dilemma.

Numbers are another language that spirit and angels speak through, seeing numbers in sequential order is a sign from the divine. Numbers such as 111, 222, 333, etc. are very prominent. There are many books and an abundance of information to seek the meanings of these numbers. If you see a number that keeps appearing it would be worth it to look it up.

Our personal energetic vibration is a critical piece when looking to trust and build the intuitive muscle. The afterlife speaks through the same communication system. We are all vibrational beings; the higher the vibrational frequency the easier it to connect and feel the afterlife. This is why healing is such an important piece of your journey to establish the new communication with your loved one on the other side. So you can have a better understanding of vibration (how or what raises your vibration frequency).

You were born with this ability to connect. I do not have extra super powers that allow me to receive spiritual information. This is a muscle that I have developed and use this muscle each day so it is strong. So please have patience with yourself as you are strengthening your own spiritual muscle. I will guide you through the process in further chapters.

Here are a few of the ways to increase your vibration frequency:

- Music
- Acceptance
- Laughing
- Nature's remedy
- Hugs and affection
- Meditation
- Opening your heart to love
- Forgiveness
- Gratitude
- Animals
- The sun
- Creativity (painting, journaling, etc.)
- Talking with caring people
- Body movement (exercise, dancing)

There are numerous ways to lift your vibration, even though you may not feel motivated to do some of these suggestions all the time. Give yourself permission, or a gentle push, to try once a day. It is important to your mental health and well being to try. You are worth the effort. When your vibrational frequency is low, you could feel tired, nausea, sluggish, and depressed. The small shifts you commit to each day become new patterns of living. You can always ask your team of angels to help give you the motivation to make you a priority. They love supporting you.

Speaking of angels...let me introduce some of the angels we will be talking about in this book.

Archangels- The archangels are magnificent spiritual beings of light and illumination. They are governed by divine will intertwined between heaven and humanity. They are more than willing to offer love, support, healing, and guidance to each of us here on Earth. They, however, cannot intervene without our permission. Archangels are the overseers of the angelic world, watching over the guardian angels, guides and other angels that are supporting our earth walk.

Archangel Michael: His color is a magnificent sapphire blue. He is the overseer and protector of the heavens and the Earth. He offers us shielding and protection; strength and courage to move through any challenges is amplified when calling on this powerful angel. I call upon Archangel Michael every day to shield and protect my energy. With his assistance, I have been able to move into the unknown areas of my life feeling safe and secure.

Archangel Raphael: This angel is emerald green and known as the healing angel. When asked, this angel can assist you with healing on the emotional and physical level. Archangel Raphael works alongside doctors, nurses, and those who work in the healing fields. I utilize the healing abilities of Raphael during my sessions. Often when someone is in pain, I ask that they be flooded with emerald green light to lift the heaviness from them so that they can feel a sense of lightness surround them. I would ask Raphael to release me from the gut-wrenching pain that I felt in my chest and allow me to go through the experience without the physical pain.

Archangel Gabriel: This white, iridescent ray of divine light is the messenger of God. He assists us with communication, writing, or speaking our truth from the heart. Calling on Gabriel can assist

28

you in healing as you have the courage to speak your loving truth, restoring balance and harmony once more in your life. This magnificent angel is no stranger to my life. I call upon him each day and while writing this book. I ask that the words flow through me with love and compassion.

Archangel Uriel: Amber light is the color of this glorious angel. Uriel assists us in clearing out the mental clutter and baggage so that we can achieve wisdom and clarity. Uriel can also assist you in bringing faith or strengthening the faith when life has weakened it. This is the first of the angels that I ever started working with. My mind was very cluttered and had trouble organizing my thoughts because of the chaos in my life. When I asked for his healing abilities to be in my life, my thoughts started to clear and small shifts of clarity began to be available to me.

Archangel Azrael: Azrael, associated with violet, means "whom helps God". Azrael assists all souls to cross over feeling the love and peacefulness of the divine so that fear and uncertainty extinguish. I am often visited by this angel during my sessions, to confirm and validate his beloved presence during the crossing over process.

Guardian Angels- Upon coming into the world, our soul is assigned two guardians to watch over our time here on our life walk. One is masculine and the other feminine to create a balance of energy. They are with us throughout our life from the moment of conception until we cross over.

Angels vibrate at a high vibrational frequency. Guardian angels can lower their frequency in order to be closer to humanity in order to oversee your journey. Unlike the other angels, Guardian Angels will not ever leave you because they are assigned to your soul. As all angels, guardians are governed by free will, free choice- the divine law. Guardian Angels have the most difficult of jobs because they watch us struggle and cannot intervene without our release of free will. They watch over us when we struggle and they celebrate our victories with us. There are specific situations when a Guardian Angel can intervene against free will, free choice. If a soul is in a situation of danger and is at risk to crossover and it is not their end date to leave their journey, they will intervene.

In sessions for parents who have lost children, I have noticed that they now have an extra guardian angel assigned to them aiding to support the emotions and give more love to them. Clients that have had a near death experience, they are assigned an extra angel to help them acclimate back into the earth walk. Near death experiences that a few of my clients shared remembered stated that they never "felt so much love and peace" and "they did not want to leave" once they returned, they felt they had a different view of their world.

If your loved one ever experienced an overdose and was brought back to life, they were given extra support coming back to help them to recover or to help strengthen them. It was another opportunity for them to move through the challenges they faced. It is difficult for our loving angels to watch us struggle knowing we are capable of accomplishing. They do not like watching any of us hurt much less the soul that they chose to guard and protect. The overwhelming feeling of helplessness and they are waiting for the release of free will to rush to the beloved side. Often in the times of deep grief, people thoughts take them into unthinkable places of contemplating suicide because the pain is so unbearable. This is not the answer; it only creates more darkness and more grief for those left behind who love you.

As I stated earlier, we have two teams of divine support. The first team is the angels and your second team is the loved ones who crossed over.

In my sessions when I am speaking to those crossed over, they rarely ever use the words "death" or "died" because they view us

30

of having a death of yesterday. In the afterlife, there is no time. So yesterday is a death to us because we cannot have it back. They are now limitless with no physical form or linear time frames. They are spirit, pure light energy.

These teams surround you every day from the heavenly realms, particularly during times of trauma and grief, where they are unconditionally shedding light and love on you. When a person leaves this earth, it is the vessel or physical body in which we lay to rest. Along with their free will free choice, they are released of any emotional or physical discomfort, and the soul is greeted by a team of angels, specifically Archangel Azrael. Azrael gently assists each soul into ascension. At this point, they will have a reunion with loved ones. When each of us crosses, anything that does not align with love, is laid to rest. The concepts of free will, illness, suffering, pain, are all laid to rest with the vessel (body) as they do not align with love. They only exist on a lower vibration frequency in the human world and cannot hold space in the pure undivine, unconditional world.

Upon returning home (this is our "Earth Journey" and the afterlife is home), the soul is greeted with extra love and support from the angels to nurture and offer love from the pain of the situation from which they came. I often tell my clients if they can envision a soldier who has been at war. That soldier is not just thrust back into society; they have a debriefing and a process to ease them back into civilian life. This transition period for the soul is supporting and nourishing the preparation for viewing their life review. Judgment does not exist in the afterlife. That is a human condition. God does not reject any child, much less one that has been suffering or hurting. Divine love is unconditional and pure.

This initial crossover is a critical point because at that moment, the soul now is fully awakened and it is witnessing the devastation that their family and friends are feeling upon discovering the news of their passing. As a soul they now are separated from the vessel, or body. As we learned previously, the vessel holds the free will. The soul is now a witness, fully awakened, and in the pure state of light and love.

They are awakened as to how much love and support they had on earth. They realize now that they were "living asleep". They refer to it as "living asleep" because they may have had moments, times of clarity but were not fully aware of what their family was going through during their active addiction. They now acknowledge how much pain everyone felt and how much time their loved ones invested in wanting them to get better. They now know that it was not just them addicted to the drug but the effects it had on all the relationships in their life. They had spent so much time focusing on feeding the beast within them or self punishing themselves for their choices that they did not recognize the full magnitude of the situation.

As your reading this, you may be getting a sick feeling in your stomach not wanting your loved one to feel helpless or guilty on the other side. Please know they are in the safest space for them to witness this because they now do not have judgment against themselves. However, they are more determined than ever to heal from the journey they had been on. The spirits refer to it as "eyes of neutrality". Neutral eyes are able to observe and understand without feeling the pain but are observers of the journey they have left. I will go into more depth with this in the later chapters on their crossing.

One mother shared this poem with me as she said it helped offer peace during her healing process.

"Took Me By The Hand"
Author Unknown

Last night while I was trying to sleep, my son's voice I did hear.
I opened my eyes and looked around but he did not appear.
He said, "Mom you've got to listen, you've got to understand
God didn't take me from you mom, he only took my hand

When I called out in pain, the instant that I died,
He reached down and took my hand, and pulled me to his side.
He pulled me up and saved me from the misery and pain
My body hurt so badly inside, I could never be the same.

My search is really over now, I've found happiness within.
All the answers to my empty dreams and all that might have been.

I love you so and miss you so, but I'll always be nearby,
My body's gone forever, but my spirit will never die.
And so you must go on now live one day at a time.
Just understand, god did not take me away from you,
He only took my hand.

Notes _____

_____

_____

_____

_____

_____

_____

_____

_____

_____

_____

_____

_____

_____

_____

_____

_____

_____

_____

_____

_____

_____

Chapter 4

Grief

"The shoe that fits one person will pinch another; there is no recipe for living that suits all cases"
C.J. Jung

There is no guide book for grief. Grief is not a natural state of being. The natural state of the soul is living in joy and love. It is important that we be able to differentiate between living in grief and missing our loved ones. Grief carries an overwhelming heaviness; a place devoid of self reflection and understanding one's own emotions and pain. The waves of grief can sneak up on you in the most unexpected moments; washing dishes, driving, and doing the daily day-to-day. Instead, missing them is a state of reflection as you learn to move into a new normal. Normal looks different now than it did in the past. The reality of missing our loved ones can be the most difficult to work through. This is because life is still in motion but the feelings of "if they were here," what would life look like?

Developing a clear understanding between the two will help you to heal. As stated earlier, missing your loved one is very different than grief. Grief is a constant pain and existence. When we accept that we can miss them and still live, it gives you the opportunity to be able to think of them without feeling the physical pain in your body associated with grief.

Even though we know death is an unavoidable reality for all of us, we set expectations or ideas of how one will or should pass. Our feelings of life being "fair" plays out. Somewhere along the line a hierarchy has been created in this world that states that the elderly should go first, believing that they have lived a long, good life and should be the first souls to cross over. In reality, each soul has its own journey and own transition point. It has very little to do with how we think it should be.

I have sat with widows and widowers who feel guilty they did not expect or plan that their partner who passed would cross first. Do not judge age or circumstances when a person should pass or feel guilty about it. For parents especially, this is most difficult to accept. Parents do not anticipate outliving their children because we have this unwritten rule in our heads that we should go before they do. But as we have learned, we all have a birth date and an end date already bestowed to us.

What Grief Looks Life

In many societies and cultures, we have been conditioned as to what grief *should* look or feel like. Know this: no one is grieving correctly or incorrectly. No one grieves like anyone else. How we can generalize something so intimate as our connections to one another or to set a standard on how grief should look is absurd.

Many of my clients express they feel guilty for finding laughter in their life again after their loved one's passing but find it exhausting to stay in the state of feeling numb. Be gentle with yourself as you make the choice to put down the weight of carrying such sadness.

Other clients have expressed feeling shame in talking about the loved one's passing because of the choices they made while living and the circumstances surrounding their loved one's passing. They feel judged and overly protective of the name of their loved one and also are protecting themselves against further judgment from others. This may be something you have either personally experienced (judgment) or you are projecting what others may be feeling about you. They have pointed out that the confusion and the emotional turmoil they have felt has left them wondering how their lives have gotten to this point. As you are moving through this emotional experience, the thought alone of outside opinions and others' perceptions of you for your loved one is an unwelcoming aspect. Many have shared feelings of anxiety and stress going into social situations. They worry about the offhand comments that they perceive as judgmental and hurtful, while that was never the intent.

Too many will suffer in silence to hide their pain so they do not make other people uncomfortable with their sadness. Human nature typically has an awkwardness surrounding death and grief. For you, it does not matter how much time passes, the reality is that no matter how much time you have had, you will always want more. The disguise of your old normal may fool some, but you cannot hide it or mask it indefinitely. Life becomes different now; not good or bad, just different. Outsiders know life will be different but they do not understand *how* this new difference changes your life.

When you are grieving, you can still teach people how to treat you. When your emotions feel raw, comments from others can feel like a dull razor blade on your skin. Speaking up for yourself is never a bad thing. In fact, the angels recognize and condone education as the best tool for teaching others how to treat you. They are beside you helping you bring awareness to people who do not understand how you feel. By staying silent, you are condoning the actions of others as appropriate.

The transition you make from losing a loved one to creating a new normal is not always an easy one no matter how your loved one passed. This is your existence and your loss; therefore, you need to do what makes you comfortable in your healing process. If you want to talk about your loved one, do it. Do not be shy or self-conscious because of how they passed. If you are not ready to talk to people about your loved one, do not feel obligated to.

If your fear of what others will say keeps you from saying anything, this is the time to respond with dignity and clarification. Here are some examples of what others say and how you could respond:

What they say:	How to respond:
"Well, they are better off now."	"I am happy they aren't in pain but I don't find comfort in not having them here."
"You have to move on."	"I don't have to do anything. Every day I practice breathing forward. Breath by breath is my current plan of healing."
"Well, when I lost [name] I did/felt…"	"While I am sorry for your loss, each loss is unique and this is different for me."

"If I were you, I would feel..."	"If you want to support me and my feelings, give me a hug, space, or a listening ear. I have enough negative thoughts in my head and don't need yours as well."
If you hear someone speaking negatively about your loved one	Speak up for your loved one. Do not sit in silence.

One mother I had visited for a session told me that she had no other option but to shift her grieving so that she was not living in a state of death every day. Each day she did one thing different than she had since the day her daughter passed. Each day she practiced small steps to celebrate her daughter's life instead. She knew, deep within her own heart, her daughter would not want her mother to live her own personal death every day.

Before going through your experience, you could only imagine, or fearfully visualize what it may feel like when death occurs, but never actually be prepared for when your worst fears have come true. As I have sat with my clients over the years, I have come to notice they all have a similar thread in their tapestries of life. While living as a family (or friend of an addict), they walk on eggshells daily. They remember the feelings of panic and the dropping of their stomach when the phone rang from an unknown number or jumping to the door when someone was knocking, silently praying it was not a police officer bringing you the news of your loved one's passing.

How are we ever to prepare for what we have never experienced, but feared and lived out mentally on a daily basis? All these projected emotions have shifted to what could happen to know what is. The feeling is different than anything you could have possibly imagined. At times, the pain seems unbearable. When these painful feelings arise, you need to breathe through them. When you hold your breath, it traps the pain- creating an energy blockage- causing you more pain. If you think of childbirth, it is in labor that you experience pain; the doctors and nurses are guiding us to breathe and push and release the force of discomfort. Breathing through the difficult moments may seem silly or ineffective, but this method helps to re-center and ground oneself in the present moment as you are opening up an energetic channel to allow the painful energy to flow through you.

Each grief is as unique as your fingerprints. It is a personal experience. Some people survive and talk about their feelings afterwards like a distant memory. Some people sit in silence and never open up about it. Others take the experience and create organizations to support the battle and to keep their loved one's name alive. There is no room for yourself or others to judge as you are living in unimaginable pain. People do not know what to do when someone they care about is grieving.

The statements, "they are in a better place," "God only takes the good ones" or "it gets better," does not add comfort. Instead, it can create agitation for those that have just lost someone. The truth is they are not trying to hurt you but people (humanity) feel uncomfortable with your pain so they search for the right words to say in hopes that it will heal or comfort you.

Nothing anyone can say is going to help fix the broken heart you have. Healing is a personal choice. If one day you may choose to stay in bed or avoid friends and family, it is perfectly acceptable; just do not make it your everyday routine. Just because you have a day of peace, does not mean you have "cured your grief." It is ok for you to have a good day. There is no timeline on your grief process. Your day can be whatever you chose to make it. With so many things are out of your control, this belongs to you.

Healing is an inside job and it requires patience and self compassion. This unwanted reality is now your new normal, so every emotion and feeling are not to be compared to life that you had in the past. You might be feeling that if I let go of the pain, it means I let go of my loved one or that the pain will come back tenfold.

Your pain places a trance like state on your world as you "get through the day." Getting through the day does not resonate with me in this time of grief. I tell clients that they are to find victory in one breath at a time. Your pain is not your new identity.

As you move through the spiral of grief you may witness each breath bringing up another emotion. According to the spirit world, the first year is usually referred to as the "fog". You may recognize this state as "what the hell just happened to me?" The mind can create mental stories about past events and rage a war of persecution onto you. It is important to try and have awareness of your thought process because this war will reside in your mind.

Often when recalling your loved one, you may find yourself remembering them pre-addiction and using this memory to create "could be" moments that are easy to drown in. This romanticized view of the person you lost can throw daggers into your healing because you are not processing the information as it occurred in reality. This is not to say you should avoid joyful memories about your loved one, but to view the events with eyes of truth.

The addiction is a painful monster and your loved one was in pain. Unfortunately, even when in recovery, the person may seem to be having great days or great moments but battling a new demon within their thoughts. Adjusting to a new normal can bring on new worries. For many addicts, their "normal" was worrying about their next fix, where to get it, and getting it without the risk of fentanyl. This lifestyle is exhausting but a very real truth to them. I hear from the addicts crossed over that they hated using the drugs and they wanted nothing more than to be free from this disease. The mind is a powerful tool for life, but it can also be a terrorist. It can terrorize your peace.

When we face the truth in our realities we then can process things differently. The word "acceptance" is a word I am sure you are all too familiar with. As a former enabler, I hated that word "acceptance". I felt like it was a cop-out, as if I was supposed to sit back and watch something that was totally unacceptable.

As my knowledge and my spiritual connection expanded, I was shown by the angels as to what find acceptance meant. It was explained to me, "Acceptance does not mean that you have to like it, but what it is." From this point of acceptance, you now ask yourself, "What do I have control over?" The answer is what you have always only had control over- your own thoughts, feelings, and actions. This is the most difficult part of the healing process because it is met with the most resistance.

I can imagine most people reading this probably have thought little of the actions in their life as they have been worried sick about the life of their loved one. This is viewed in the afterlife as a "double grief." You are grieving the physical person who has passed and now the grief of time spent worrying. Your time was spent worrying because you were living a double life- working during the day and searching facilities, hospitals, and streets for your loved one by night. Worrying became a full time job on its own. Your past experience has not been easy or pleasant; it has monopolized your past existence.

Now that you have time, it seems like a sentence and not a gift. The loss of time and the fear of calendars as the mind wanders into, "How am I going to do this?" You may have thoughts of wanting to abandon holidays, birthdays, or anniversaries of their passing. They do not wish for your life to stop and for joyous moments of celebration to bring a halt to their memory or name. They want you to make an intentional commitment to self-love and healing. They want you to refocus the energy from pain, shock, or trauma into a slow, steady process of believing that life and peace are possible again. Your time and energy has been exhausted worrying about your loved one. Think back to all your shared conversations on belief and hope that they are healing in addiction and live healthy lives. This, ironically, is their message to you. Let go of the addictive behavior of worrying and pain.

One of the most powerful breakthroughs that I have witnessed many times during a session is when the gut wrenching cry follows the statement, "I feel guilty for feeling relief on some level because now I know where they are. They are free of the emotional pain and torture they lived."

Now your loved one has full access to the ramifications of addiction on their family. As spirit, they can be with each member, encouraging them to heal as they recognize each family member owns their own state of grief. Each has had their own perception of the process that has lead them to the loss. The weight of this loss can sever family relationships and dynamics while others choose to bond together and move through it as a unit. Blame and judgment have no winner in this battle. Loved ones crossed now want to help you to heal the resentments and relationship strains that may have been impacted by the addiction. They do not want to watch their families being torn apart any further. There has been enough grief.

Notes _____

_____
_____
_____
_____
_____
_____
_____
_____
_____
_____
_____
_____
_____
_____
_____
_____
_____
_____
_____
_____
_____

Chapter 5

The Other Side

Is there a Heaven and what does it look like?

Before going into the details of your loved ones and what happens, let's dial back to where we go and what it is like. In almost every session, I get asked, "Is there a heaven?" and "What is it like?" Being raised Catholic, in my mind, I had envisioned it to be a glorious place with angels, fluffy clouds, harps, large white columns, and big pearly gates. I guess you could say it looked like an old Roman painting. However, now that I share a workspace with the divine, I see a vastly different existence.

If you call it Heaven, the Afterlife, the Other Side, or the Universe it is all the same: it is more a choice of verbiage. When I have been shown what it looks like, the universe has no beginning and no end but endless creation. Close your eyes and imagine the night's sky filled with millions of lights and stars. Since I personally never have crossed over, I can tell you how spirit describes it to me. I have asked many spirits and angels to describe to me what heaven feels like. Their response is this:

The afterlife is coming home. Home to where there is no pain or duality within ourselves or the outside world. Upon crossing I felt a warmth move through my body as I was lifted up into a light so bright the human eyes would be blinded with a glimpse of it. The feeling of love filled me so deeply that the human experience would almost be unable to comprehend the feeling of it. Love is a pure, unconditional source.

Many have said to take the most magical love-filled moment and times it by infinity. As a medium, I have been brought to tears with an overwhelming sensation of pure love when connecting in some sessions. It has been described as a feeling of peace and tranquility that now they are a part of.

Other clients that I have spoken to described their near death experience as euphoric; they felt so loved and safe that when they were told they could not stay in the warmth of the afterlife and that they needed to return back to their lives, they felt an overwhelming sorrow upon returning to this plane. This was not because they didn't love their families or have an appreciation for their life, but to be secured in a cocoon of pure joy and bliss. It was described as an all-knowing acceptance of this return home and that they knew internally that they would not be leaving their family but viewing them from new lenses. There is an understanding that they will always being with them as they move throughout the day and eventually, their families would be ok.

There are many levels to the afterlife. For the purpose of this explanation, so the human mind can comprehend, we can call them classrooms. The soul has to learn and continue to grow whilst in the afterlife, and to do so it to will go into a different classroom. This is not to say they stay in these classrooms indefinitely. They can move freely through the classrooms. This could really be its own book, but to help put this in perspective I will share a little to help you understand what they are and consist of.

There are many levels to the afterlife and its classrooms. To reiterate, this is our Life Walk. As we recognize it, schools support learning and growth. If the soul has completed many of the predestined developmental lessons that the soul chose to learn here on Earth to support its own growth and progress, than it is vibrationally aligned with kindred souls to move into a classroom. Within these classrooms, they are supported on their vibrational levels to help flourish further.

All classrooms vary and hold certain communities based around their energetic alignment to lessons. Everyone in these classrooms vibrates on the same level. We can move freely throughout the levels to reunite with loved ones and friends that we knew here on the Earth Plane or others prior to this lifetime. We eventually come back to one another but we do not feel the need to stay with one another like we do in the physical world. On this earthly plane, we live territorially. The idea of belonging to each other is strictly a human belief. In the afterlife, a soul has complete understanding as they are now infinite wisdom and pure love. Understanding a oneness that when souls come together to learn, build, and assist us on this plane with our lessons. The soul craves knowledge and this is what is offered within the classrooms. Upon returning home, the soul understands love from a higher perspective. The soul encourages us to step away from distortions of the mind and pain of the physical world by living in grief, guilt, or pain. The soul encourages us to feel and heal with confidence. The souls of our loved ones are waiting for us when it is our time to go. Upon meeting up, we come together to learn lessons and build together again.

Love is the only energy that can exclusively live in both realms. We have the ability to experience this depth of love here on Earth but the free will of the human often puts conditions or labels around it. On the other side, we recognize that we are all created from the great source light of God, with each soul representing the light. The God in you is the God in all of us. This is where pure unconditional love comes from.

Crossing over into Heaven

The angels recognize that this newly crossed soul has had many struggles during their earthly walk. The first phase of transition from the earthly realms to the other side is very nurturing and gentle. Each soul is unique and the transition of the soul is equally unique in its return home. The angels have guided me through the process of what the soul experiences during a cross over.

My experiences are all I can speak with confidence, as I have been shown throughout my many years in practice. As in any career, people may have the same degree, licensure, or job title but have their own way of doing their job to complete their work. It is the same as in my world within my career. Each medium or spiritual guide has their own unique signature as to how they receive and deliver messages to their guests.

I have met with thousands of families who have experienced a loved one's passing caused by an overdose. I have reunited them with their loved ones on the other side. In many times of trauma, those who pass from suicide or overdose are treated with more tenderness and nurturing than usual. I have included suicide with this because the soul does not make the decision to live through suicide as a "life purpose lesson". It is of the free will of the human mind that makes the choice. It is not a selfish act but a lack of self-love. Those who possess a deeper understanding of their value and self-acceptance are less likely to harm themselves with destructive behaviors. When overdoses come through, often they will share that it was a game of Russian Roulette in not knowing what was in the substance they were using.

When your loved one crosses, they compare it to a soldier that has been away at war. When the soldier returns home, the soldier must first go through a debriefing and a transition period prior to going back into civilian life. Similar to the soul that is newly crossed, in session it has been described as a triage unit, when you go to the emergency room you are being evaluated-you are in the hospital but not yet assigned a bed or room. This evaluation point is critical for the soul's orientation back into the spirit world. This "triage unit" is designed to prepare them to acclimate back into the spirit realm with feelings of love and support in order to manage the upcoming life review.

The life review is to showcase the life that the soul has lived during the human journey. They witness the moments from the womb till passing. They witness how many accomplishments they had experienced during their time here. These moments include all the little victories such as them learning to walk, read, or run (accomplishments that normally would be taken for granted) to all the joyful experiences they did successfully. The review allows them to see life through your eyes and the eyes of people they shared experiences with. This is a gift for the soul's growth on the other side from there they can grow and evolve. Remember there is no judgment in the afterlife.

When connecting into the afterlife, I explain the process during my sessions so that the client can feel the experience through me. It is easy to tell someone but to truly understand the why and how of this living miracle is where the healing can take place. I explain that when I connect into the afterlife, it is like walking into a crowded restaurant that you own. These are all your angels, guides, and loved one from many generations that are all supporting you from their end. When I first enter, I act as a news reporter on the scene live and I report the news to you as I receive it. When I am meeting your loved one, they are a spirit/soul. It is not the physical body that I see but I feel them and then through my third eye or brow chakra (the inner sight we call it). I get words and pictures, and then I start the conversation as if I was talking to you. Depending on the number of spirits present, it may take me a few minutes to dial into their frequency. Remember they are energy or full light beings now; we are energy so it is like turning into their soul station.

As for communicating with them, we will cover this a little later in the book. Communication between us and them comes in many forms; therefore, it needs its very own chapter.

Whether you are a true believer in God or have faith in a higher power, agnostic, or atheist, God believes in you. When we come into the world we have all the tools and understanding that is required to do the earth walk. For example, children are filled with curiosity and wonder as they move through the stages of their growth. Children have an exceptional view into the afterlife by sensing and seeing spirit because they have just come from the heavenly realms to the earth. Around 10 or 11 years old, children start to discover their sense of independence and build new identities at school, which softens the connection. As you age, you have experiences that might not seem fair or that have created a hurt or a lack of self-confidence. Most beliefs in self-worth start from childhood and it can be very small statements made that carry a lasting effect. No matter how much we love someone, we cannot always teach them, to accept themselves.

It is often that people struggling become angered at God or want to blame God for the way things are unfolding. It is not God's doing. This is all part of "free will, free choice," a very sacred choice we made in coming to this life. God would never send us here to struggle. Instead, you are here to learn and grow on a soul level. God does not reject or shun us for being angry or upset with Him. The person hurting is given more love, angels, and compassion. It is up to them to allow this love in. When someone crosses, all the earthy questions become clear. They understand that they had the skills, the will and the courage to change and manifest any situation.

Being a professional medium for many years means there will be questions and inquiries about the afterlife on many different levels. People want to know the answer to the question, "Where do bad people go when they die?" For the purposes of this book, I am only going to dive into the question based on overdose cases. I am not referencing any other type of ethical infraction we might come across here on this life walk.

When being asked to explain if someone is "good" or "bad", I have to first explain that everything is made up of energy. As spirit, we are working through a human experience. We hold a vibrational body, as well as, the vibrations of our emotions, thoughts/beliefs, and our actions. Whether they are positive or negative vibrations, they still emanate out of our beings into the universe. This is our part of our personal perception of how we take in energy and release it.

What energy we receive from others is what we hold as our perception of them. So for example, if we feel negative energy off of someone, we tend to automatically assume they are a "bad" individual. However, the angels would rather us let this notion go. Instead, they would rather have us understand it is just energy and not necessarily the whole of that individual. On this Earth Plane, we have this preset understanding of what is "good" and "bad"; therefore, we base our belief system as our judgment system for others around us. The divine does not hold the same judgment system that we do here on Earth. When they see us, it is not so "black and white" or "good or bad". They want to empower us to own our choices and rather than labeling ourselves. The stigma of what an addict is or who they are can be perceived as bad. It is not that they are not bad, but they are making bad decisions. You know that they are struggling internally, but it this is not who they are at a core level.

When an individual is under the influence, it greatly shifts their vibrations between the physical body and the soul. The soul vibrates at a higher capacity, so when a substance interferes with that, it makes it even more difficult for the soul to utilize its full strength or power. With this loss of empowerment, it creates a lower vibration with the physical body leading to feelings of self punishment or blame. It is not God, or the divine, creating blame. Blame is a human emotion. That being said, the more they feed the addiction beast, the more troubled they feel. This then lowers the physical vibration to the point it does not match the soul's vibration. This is where there is a sense of loss and detachment.

To help an individual come back to that attachment where the physical body and soul are aligned vibrationally, they need to release the negative beliefs about themselves to then rebuild from there. By releasing blame and letting go of the addiction, they restore the higher vibration pieces at a time until both the physical body and soul are closer in vibration. At this point, they align closer and heal together to heal the individual.

Should this not occur and an overdose happens, that individual is still greeted by a team of angels who do love and support them unconditionally. This is when they are brought in with extra love and compassion to help restore their soul's vibration now that the physical body is no longer attached. It is from there, they go into the classrooms and learn new lessons.

Notes _____

_____

_____

_____

_____

_____

_____

_____

_____

_____

_____

_____

_____

_____

_____

_____

_____

_____

_____

_____

Chapter 6

Their Passing- Before, During, and After

When given the chance...

On this earthly realm we are driven by time, rushing through it, praying for more of it, but many of us are absent of just being in the moment. Being "in the moment" means taking time to calm your thoughts. It can be anything from the stresses of living in the past or anxieties about the future. Being in the now of the moment on this realm is similar to being in the afterlife.

When we come into the world with our soul charts, we have a birth date and an end date, which are predestined. On our soul chart, we also have multiple exit points. The soul may have a near death experience where it will witness what is called a review point. During this review point, those addicted may see a future where they are living clear, clean, and sober; while others may witness if they stay on their current path, they will not heal. Some may witness how capable they are and always have been. To shift from the negativity that fills their minds and bodies by witnessing in this review, all the wonderful things that they have done since birth and all the successes that they have already lived.

Not all souls have the same experiences due to the uniqueness of each journey. When a soul is in a near death situation, the soul is then shown a movie clip and not the full life review. It is a future excerpt of their life moving forward; what their life would hold if they continued on the same path and if they choose another path.

I have spoken to souls on the other side who have chosen to stay in the afterlife when given exit points. This is due to the fact they have struggled for years in this living hell within their addiction and in their minds; they have had numerous overdoses and were brought back to life again; or they are tired and crave peace. Their intentions were not to harm their families any further but to have peace and to give peace to everyone else. They understand that their families would fight the fight just to have them back for one last hug. The souls that have overdosed share the details of how now they can see the truth now that they are awakened as they walked the earth in a sleep like addicted state.

Do they feel pain, fear, or suffering?

When the moment of passing is in front of you, everything happens quickly and all time conception vanishes. It has been described to me as a euphoric feeling of weightlessness and warmth. All the earthly discomforts and heaviness associated with them no longer exist. A sense of calm and tranquility fills the soul as it remembers the truth in whom and why they came into their life. Every soul comes into the world with two cord attachments; the umbilical cord that is cut at birth and our soul cord that dissolves at our passing.

Imagine a kite with a string attached to the soul cord. Upon passing, the soul is greeted by angels helping them to release any earthly attachments or energies that may still be attached. It is here the soul and human vessel are no longer one. Your loved one is going through the experience all while not feeling pain or discomfort as their soul is moving forward into the afterlife.

Often I hear from the other side that they witness their passing from an aerial view of what is transpiring. In many cases of an overdose passing, the spirits have described to me that they feel great compassion and freedom from the life they lived while living addicted or in a relapse mindset. That the pain they felt everyday or that moment when they chose to use was excruciating mentally. Unfortunately, a feeling they were too familiar with. However, now they are at peace.

Fear is another condition that does not exist when we cross over. To have fear is to be human. Once the soul exits the physical body, they do not feel fear any longer. They feel a lightness and warmth come over them as they watch their light (soul) leave the physical body they once occupied.

A small blessed message that has been shared with me is that many cases of addiction overdose are the person just slipping into a sleep-like state into spirit. The physical body is the house of the soul. When the soul exits the physical body, it does not have emotions or feel physical pain no matter the situation.

Many families that I sit with share that they have been haunted with their thoughts at night thinking about the situation that their loved one passed in. Their minds are filled with sadness and worry wondering if their last breaths here were filled with fear and asking if they were afraid. Please rest your mind and know that your loved one was nurtured, supported and transitioned gracefully with ease.

We do not suffer when we pass. Suffering is a human experience; a perception held by those witnessing, not the soul experience. The light of the soul can be dimmed when the human is making choices that are against the original assignment of the soul and its purpose here.

Just a few things that dim your light can be:
- Self Doubt
- Abusive Situations
- Lack of Self Love
- Others Thoughts/Opinions of Us
- Negative Thinking
- Substance Abuse

Your loved one has mentally and emotionally suffered with the battle within themselves. The person who you loved has faded in and out of their own lives depending on how long they have struggled with their addiction. The addiction is the manipulator who looks like the person you loved but is a thief of their light. The suffering that they experienced was the everyday mental battle with themselves, feeling as though they would never find their way out of their rock-bottom or into a place of forgiveness and self-worth.

As outsiders, we can view someone from where they are and what they look like on the outside and create judgment based on that appearance. What we view on the outside is not always what is on the inside. It is as if you are driving down a beautiful, well-kept street and view a beautiful home. The house could be immaculate in every way, but we do not see the inside from the street. The insides could be destroyed, gutted, or even empty. It is all about perception. Not everything we see on the outside is complimentary to the inside. Making the assumption that everything is well with someone because they look put together and clean can confuse family and friends when a relapse occurs. What was going on inside of their loved one was not reflective on the outside.

Were they alone or was someone there with them?

When we are crossing, we are not alone. No matter how isolated or alone we felt in the physical world or if we pass while alone, we are always divinely supported. Their personal guardian angels have been with them since conception and step up into action as they assist the soul into the transition process, showing them with unconditional love and warmth. Your loved ones previously passed can spend time and visit with your loved one as they transition. During sessions we will see a reunion of families come together to surround you and comfort you offering messages of support.

It is only on this plane where the feelings of not good enough or the need to isolate oneself exists. When our loved ones cross, it is the highest intention for all souls to feel loved and supported as they transcend into the afterlife. The feelings of emotional suffering happen here on Earth for those left behind.

As you are trying to process the loss, the mind can often becomes a script writer creating scary and horror films as you play out movies of you projecting what they felt like. It's only natural to go into the worst case scenario based upon the circumstances of their passing. The mind is replaying what we think happened, but each time it plays out, the details become more intense and gruesome. This leaves you in a state of inner worry and guilt; feeling sick to your stomach. Since we personally have not crossed over, we are left to fill in the blanks. After reading this, it is now up to you to cancel, clear, delete these mental movies that are keeping you in a space of pain. I share an affirmation with my clients who have problems shutting off these thoughts.

Should you worry about your loved one, simply say, "My loved one (fill in their name) is safe and at peace." This affirmation can be repeated over and over again to help replace the thoughts of pain and suffering that we fear they went through. Change happens with subtle gentle shifts of our perception and thoughts. As you practice this affirmation you will start to notice the negative thoughts and assumptions will lessen as you become more aware of the positive thoughts being created by this affirmation. The negative assumptions will dissolve, because as you repeat your affirmation, it slowly becomes something you believe and trust. Your loved one is safe and at peace.

What are they doing now?

This question has many moving parts because there are billions of souls on the other side. I have often asked this question to my angels and my loved ones crossed over. They are not sitting around eating bon bons, that's for sure. They are assisting humanity to become aligned with the natural vibration of peace and love, as we intended to live. As a whole, our planet is globally unbalanced and the souls see this and now can offer assistance from where they are. They are assisting us in our personal worlds as we grow through our day, but since they no longer have a physical body they can move freely to many places at once.

This life is like earth school, where we have many opportunities to learn and grow as our life charts noted. You learned about this in earlier chapters about the journey to this earth walk and the life charts we create. Some souls are in classrooms on the other side learning how to guide other souls going through experiences down here. Some souls are overseers of children and animals. Some govern the land and the seas. Others will reincarnate back into the earthy realms bringing with them the knowledge they have been given on the other side. Reincarnation is not an overnight experience. This happens over lifetimes. Remember there is no time in the afterlife; time is only conditional on the earthly realms. Food and water are nonexistent due to the fact it is the human vessel that needs these to live, the soul lives and breathes off of love and wisdom. Your loved one will always be with you, so do not be afraid or worried that you may be bothering them or taking them away from something more important. They are with you.

Notes _____

_____

_____

_____

_____

_____

_____

_____

_____

_____

_____

_____

_____

_____

_____

_____

_____

_____

_____

_____

_____

_____

Chapter 7

Soul Vision

Their Views and Emotions from the Other Side

Emotions are instinctive and intuitive feelings as distinguished from reasoning and knowledge. Pixar's film *Inside Out* gives us an animated look into emotions and how to deal with them. But what does this mean for those who no longer possess the physical form? Just like we react to those around us, they too feel and react to us.

Emotions can be felt and experienced but not to the degree that we physically and mentally handle them. In the physical form, we can be brought to tears of joy or grief. We can feel our hearts race with thrills or fear. We can shake with excitement or anger. Mentally we have the ability to get so caught up in our emotional feeling that we lose track of the world around us or tasks we need to accomplish the next steps. Mentally, we can fall victim to such sadness that we fail to pick ourselves back up.

For souls who have passed on to the afterlife, it is very different than what we are familiar with. For them, they can energetically feel our vibrations. This means they can feel and understand us as energy; however, they will not physically feel it and mentally they will not get caught up in the moment or situation. It is our emotions that allow us to get caught up in the everyday situations.

Perspectives change once we adjust our point of view. This is no different for those who have passed. When we cross over, we see the same situation from a different point of view. Earlier I explained that emotions will be different once we pass, but so is our view on life. So how does their view change on the life they lived and how we are now?

Higher Range of Vision

Souls crossed can sense our emotions here in the physical world based off the vibrations we give off. We are all energetic beings, doing the physical experience. Everything is energy and the soul is a pure source of energy. They are pure vibrational frequencies and we are all transmitters of vibrations by nature. Just as music is vibration and rhythm, we are as well. Think about it this way, when listening to a radio station and you are not a fan of the song selection playing, you can change the station. This is the same correlation to the vibration of our emotions; we are able to change the station to find the melody we harmonize with.

Souls can sense a range of emotions, including anger, sadness, and helplessness. The lower vibrational feelings of sadness, depression, hopelessness, and pain are all felt by our loved ones. This state can make you feel paralyzing and dark emotionally. Understand these are not your natural vibrations and it is why they are encouraging the healing process to begin or continue. They radiate divine love and the emotions that they surround us with are always in a pure state of love and compassion. It is their desire that we show ourselves the same love and compassion. High vibrational emotions are very different frequencies than the feelings of pain or helplessness in the circumstances you are now living. They can sense this and are by your side trying to give you signs that they are with you supporting you.

Like I said before, our emotions can be experienced in a multitude of vibrations. There is nothing wrong with looking back on situations and learning from them; however, when we play the "What If" game, we only create havoc within our own mind. It is only mental warfare against ourselves when we build scenarios with different outcomes. It only attacks the mind over and over again assisting in bringing your vibration lower and holding your healing hostage. Learning acceptance (not liking what happened but seeing the reality of the situation) is the opportunity to take a step in another direction outside of the mental war zone and to rise above our lower vibrations. Acceptance helps us feel without the discomfort and pain.

Our vibration is the universal language of both worlds. Our loved ones know that when you raise your vibration in your physical body and mind, it will strengthen your ability to feel, sense, and connect with them with more ease. Upon entering the afterlife, they have been released from the mental/emotional struggles from the disease and "demons" within themselves.

Addiction is a thief of the light. With the light, we are able to navigate and overcome obstacles in our path. When low vibrational substances are continuously used over time, it pushes the light out from our souls. With a lack of light, it is an invitation for the dark energies, or "demons" as the addicts call it, to infiltrate the addict and take control. The soul struggles to thrive in a low, vibrationally dense area.

These dark energies can be viewed as vultures that prey on people and their emotions. Addiction does not discriminate anyone and freely recruits people of all ages, races, and backgrounds. The darkness of addiction feeds off pain; therefore the more people in pain, the more it has to take. As the darkness penetrates the soul where the light once held space, it starts to manipulate the addict's decision whole being. When I see someone in active addiction or high, I see swarms of what would look like bees all over them. This is what alters their personalities to do unthinkable things to feed the dark beast.

When driving through particular neighborhoods, I send love out in waves. By sending love out, it helps give the soul room to let light in. People who make passing judgments or comments about addiction, this is a factor in feeding the darkness. Low vibrations attract low vibrations. This is partly why recovery is so fragile. The dark energies that had been controlling the addict for so long can be moved out. They will still linger, waiting for the opportunity to launch a mental assault on their host once again when they find a momentary weak spot.

When clients ask me, what happened or why it happened, this very reason is why it is so difficult to explain and rationalize.

Thoughts and feelings can be fleeting. Emotions can be heavy and choices can be made in a split second of darkness. While I can see the light in people, I will not be ignorant to the darkness that is present in our world. Life is polarized with the light and darkness, day and night. It is about balance.

As you read through this section, you might find yourself relating or find that you are having "ah-ha" moments. There is no denying you have lived firsthand the invasion of the darkness that resided within your loved one or yourself. The darkness is a homewrecker without any apologies. The darkness that resided within is the reason why your loved one would often manipulate you for love, money, attention, or help. The manipulator will resemble your loved one in looks and sound, but it is actually the darkness that has taken the wheel. You were not necessarily fighting your loved one. You fought the beast within them. Now in the afterlife, they can see the situation for what it was and this is their reason for why they so desperately want and desire you to heal.

Think for a moment about your neighbor's home. You cannot see what is happening on the inside unless you have access to enter. Our physical bodies are our homes. Our "homes" are decorated by our thoughts and feelings as furniture and knick-knacks decorate any house. As witnesses to our loved ones, we can often get confused by the outside appearance of the house instead.

In sessions, I will frequently hear, "I don't understand. They were doing so well/They were getting help." This is an example of seeing the exterior of the house and making assumptions of what emotions were decorating their insides. It is as if you drove past the same house on the street and guessed the color of the bathrooms or what type of cabinets are in the kitchen based on the outside appearance of the house. It does not work that way. It will be emotionally overload by asking "why". Asking the "why" of things does not bring peace. Instead it pushes it violently away. Remember, we only have control over our own actions and thoughts. Until we can walk in someone else's shoes, we will not understand the "why" of their choices.

There is no denying addiction is painful for everyone involved; it creates an emotional tsunami in life. There is turbulence in dealing with and doing everything to fight for a life. There is turbulence in the day to day love, frustration, fear and confusion while the addict is active. Although situations will vary from person to person, often clients will tell me they feel they did not have time to exhale or heal from the heightened emotions they endured before their loved one's passing. These emotionally inflamed situations wreak havoc on our physical, emotional, and spiritual being.

Those crossed have unconditional love and full access to the heaviness of the emotions you feel. They also acknowledge the emotions you felt when they lived. They understand your current emotional state is based off of frustration and pain by the situation and outcome. They know you acknowledge the disease for what it was that assisted and ended their life. They do not want you to suppress your feelings and throw everything under the umbrella, living in sadness and despair for eternity. Spirit wants you to fully feel all the emotions.

Each loss is unique; addiction loss has its own unique story. Some families may be blaming themselves for tough love while others may be blaming themselves for not Initiating or enforcing boundaries. There is no rhyme or reason to addiction or why someone was clean and chose to use "out of the blue". Sadness and despair is just one layer of grief. It has many layers; anger being one of them. Being angry at them for becoming addicted, angry at their dealer, angry at the system- whatever it may be- they want you to feel all the emotions in order to heal them.

Now that they are all-knowing and all-seeing, they have new perspectives on all things. Not only do they not want you to spend sleepless nights blaming everyone or anything for their death, but they want you to release any pain or anxiety as they see how it can affect your emotional, mental and physical health. Spirit understands all human emotions now and is encouraging us to face the emotions to release them from our bodies.

How Do They Feel About...

New Relationships/Love

If you have lost a partner or spouse, spirit wants nothing more than for you to find healthy love and partnership- no matter what type of relationship it is. These relationships can be friendly, working, or even romantic relationships. Jealousies, and the feelings of territorial love, do not exist on the other side. They wish for you to heal and work on yourself before jumping into something, or to someone else, that is not completely healthy for you. Love is supposed to be an easy flow with harmony. It's not supposed to be difficult or painful. When your heart is hurting, it is difficult to think of being able to love again. Be patient and open with yourself, and find self love to be able to trust that love does not leave you or is filled with pain or chaos.

The love you had for them does not extinguish, but you can create a new space within your heart to love someone else. They do not want you to feel any type of emptiness, longing, or missing pieces. Often times when speaking to spirits, they will say they are instrumental in sending people our way to partner with. They find someone to help you in ways they may not have been able to. Your happiness creates a lift in your vibrations so it is easier to sense that loved one closer to you once again.

Their Resting Place

Not only do they want you to find new relationships, they equally do not want anything to hold you back from experiencing new things in life. When it comes to you visiting their graves or holding on to their belongings, spirit realm has no connection to anything tangible or material possessions once they have crossed over. Their only connected by the love they share here. In both realms, love has the most value and wealth.

Graves are for the living and spirit does not linger where their physical bodies are laid to rest. They are connected externally to the love that they shared here. Should you find solace and comfort in going to the grave, they encourage you to do what is best for you. Instead, if you chose to have a space in your home or yard a dedication space they will be with you and hear you speaking with them.

If you went through cremating your loved one, the same still holds true. Making the decision to spread their ashes in a favorite space or to wear cremation piece is still supported if that is what you need to heal. Those who choose to wear cremation pieces are able to hold onto that loved one- sometimes in a literal form. They understand the need for the closeness and support that as well.

The souls are connected to the love that they shared here. This renders money, possessions, and materials moot. The spirits do not want us to make museums out of there old rooms or feel sadness in going into spaces they had once occupied. They do not want us to feel like getting rid of things that no longer serve us is disrespectful either. Instead, they want you to be happy and to never hold yourself hostage in a state of living grief in the name of them.

For those that contemplate moving or relocating, this can be very difficult. If you have a home and you love it, then stay. If you have a home and are afraid that the memories of your loved one crossed will dissolve, know that is not true. They want you to feel comfort, the compassion they have for you is abundant and support healthy decisions that you make.

This goes for memorabilia as well. If there is a piece of clothing, piece of jewelry, or memorabilia that you wear for them, they love it. Sharing their material items with people in remembrance is always supported. Many families feel a sense of comfort lying in the bed of their loved ones or smelling the scent on the clothes they once wore. It is a highly sensitive and personal decision on how you choose to keep things and spaces that are sacred to you.

For those that do not find comfort or need to hold on to material possessions, do not feel guilty or shamed in getting rid of things. This is part of your healing too. Some may judge or think it is disrespectful, but they are not in your shoes and they are feeling with their own human emotions. When parting with items, it might help break the cords that still attach you to a negative emotion or situation. The souls who have passed do not feel hurt or saddened by your decision. They support you and your happiness. The same goes for purging items. If throwing items out or donating helps you heal, they will support you in this too.

Notes _____

_____

_____

_____

_____

_____

_____

_____

_____

_____

_____

_____

_____

_____

_____

_____

_____

_____

_____

_____

Chapter 8

Release and Breathe

One Breath at a Time

While we are learning death is not as final as we have always understood it to be, it can still feel finite and cut off. What we considered to be our normal family dynamic, living arrangements, or daily order will change for better or worse. Change is always inevitable. It depends on the individuals, the family ties, and the situation in which change falls on them. Families can either flock together and heal together or they can disconnect and heal (or not heal) separately.

When a family member passes, it is not uncommon that I hear of the discord between different family members. Some parents did not see eye-to-eye on how to deal with the situation or addicted individual. One parent may have felt that tough love and discipline were the way to force a healthy change, while the other parent would be willing to do anything or even permit the behavior just to keep them around. Disagreements on how to deal with a situation can cause discord in the family ties.

Siblings have been known to get wrapped up in this disagreement as well. Some siblings get angry with parents or other family members for their ways of dealing with the situation, holding them to different standards, or even failing to acknowledge them while dealing with the sibling who was addicted. Siblings are not immune to feeling love for each other, but feelings of jealousy, resentment, and judgment can interfere in the other family relationships.

Family members not in the immediate family unit or friends can also be affected. Because the one they loved is being driven by the addiction, they could possibly fear judgment or isolation for associating with them or having them around. Some may choose to put distance between the addicted individual and themselves for self preservation or to keep their emotions guarded. It is not that they do not harbor love for them. It is more about the exercise of personal boundaries and their comfort level. In many cases, after trying to get that person help and encourage change might lead to explosive behaviors or disagreements in which case distance is put to keep the peace or to keep the fighting to a minimum.

It is not uncommon for family members and friends to make drastic changes while those addicted were still living. Some members may have felt and made the personal decision to just walk away from all of it. For some people, hurting on a daily basis because of one person's choices can hurt worse than staying around. Self preservation or their own personal sense of value leads them to retreat in another direction. Feeling the need to detach does not make you a bad, cold-hearted person. Detaching with love is a personal choice to not have contact with someone that is hurting themselves and you.

When the news of their passing comes to you, most often the feelings of anguish and questioning your decision to put distance between you and them are the first to come up. After the exhaustion of campaigning for their healing, the endless battles, and constant worry, all the hoping, begging, and praying for your loved ones recovery now seems pointless, wasted, or unaccounted for. Most of the time, healing resentment and blame are the first words that are shared from the afterlife. They do not wish the family to feel anymore loss than they have lived. They wish for you to find unity within the family and try and create a space where everyone can heal. They support healing individually and as a group.

The suffering does not end after an overdose. For anyone, blame can be a prominent emotion afterwards. Blame is assigning responsibility for any fault or wrongdoing. Whether the blame is directed at one another, at the addicted individual, or even ourselves, it can occur at any time. Some people need to feel like assigning blame will help fix or reason their anger, frustrations, resentment, or sadness. Blame only creates more tension and blockage towards healing.

I have sat with families and each member had a different response to the addiction and acceptance after the passing. Each of us grieves differently based upon your personal relationships. Some of the hardest conversations to have with yourself, is an honest one.

Speaking from your heart can be challenging. Releasing the mental chatter of what you could have done or what you could have said differently would not change the outcome. It was their disease. Whatever the choices you made in setting boundaries did not create them to use; their addiction did that. When you are honest about the facts, even though it is difficult, it will help bring you into a state of acceptance to be able to reconcile your thoughts.

When I have asked the spirits about this viewpoint they have offered an interesting perspective:

> **Colleen**- *Why do some families resist the healing process or accepting that healing is possible?*
>
> **Spirit**- *We see that the addiction has spread to our families and how they have now become addicted to the pain of this disease and attempting to help us get better in the name of love. Pain is something that has been a constant in their lives since the news of addiction came into their lives. Now that we have crossed, the pain they carry can now be justified by the death. The addiction to pain seems as difficult and foreign to break away from as becoming sober and moving through recovery was to us. Even though we hated the disease and truly wanted to be better, the idea was difficult and seemed unreachable long term. We are committed to supporting our loved ones and helping them to heal into a new normal*

Colleen*- Thank you, I did not look at the state of
pain as an addiction but can see fully how it can
be defined as a state of being. We do not go into
life preparing for such deep pain or even feel
that we could endure it.*

I said earlier, and multiple times before, they simply want your happiness. Do not be afraid that moving into the next chapter of your life that will somehow be a sign of disrespecting or forgetting them. They know you love them as they love you. The idea that healing is somehow disrespectful is solely based off of human conditioning. We are not taught how to experience intense grief in a healthy manner.

As we have learned, pain is a thief of the peace and it is up to you to shift your perception based off what you have learned. You can now take an empowered position in your healing.

Breathing with Outsiders Looking In

Clients often ask me, "When it comes to talking to people, how should I bring it up without feeling shame or judgment?" I tell them, just to talk. Do not feel the need to hide your loved one. They were more than their addiction. You knew them as so much more than just their addiction and it is perfectly acceptable to still love them for who they were.

People fear being judged and isolated in society because addiction frowned upon and seen as morally flawed. Some might suggest that person was not raised properly if they turned to abusing substances or how that person was clearly a bad person because they made those choices. Ignorance is a blissful place for many, but you do not need to take on their lack of compassion as another punch to your heart. Most people will not understand what you are going through because they have not gone through it themselves.

The stigma of addiction is a remark to ignorance and a lack of information. Everyone is at risk of this epidemic; it is not just a stereotype or specific group of people. When talking to someone who obviously seems to have little compassion or empathy, I often respond to their opinions with the quote, "I believe you believe that." This shuts down the negativity and pursuit of authority over you and your feelings.

That being said, you do not need to defend why you love who you lost or yourself, why you loved them, or why you took the actions and made decisions that you did. You do not need to justify anything to anyone. They were your loved one be it parent, sibling, spouse, child, family member, or friend.

Naturally, I am a defender to those who are mistreated and not shown compassion and have been this way since I was a child. My inner warrior awakens when I see people quietly dying inside because they fear being judged by people who do not understand. Judgment is a lack of understanding and open mindedness. When people judge, it is something in them they have not dealt with in themselves.

When discussing your loved one with them, talk about them and be proud of your role as mother, father, husband, wife, etc. No one has the right to judge you unless you allow them to. They had beautiful qualities and by nature were filled with love. When you talk about your loved ones lost, it draws them closer to you and you can start to feel their presence more. They love when you talk about them or converse with them.

Your loved one was sacred to you and do not allow a window of difficulty become their story. You have a right to talk about them. You have a right to share their story and you have a right to do so without feeling guilty or as if you are dealing with your own grief incorrectly. You have enough on your plate already. Breathe on and talk openly and lovingly about the person you love and miss.

I love learning about my clients loved ones and hearing the stories about them; it is beautiful. If you want to share a story or a picture of your loved one(s), tag me @othersideofaddiction on Instagram or the hashtag #othersideofaddiction.

Releasing Guilt

You have held on to so much. Holding on to guilt does nothing for you, your family, or your loved one. Guilt is the beast that plays puppet to the ego. Guilt is defined as "the fact of having committed a specified or implied offense or crime". Feelings are not crimes and so they should not be punished as such. Guilt is simply the feeling of not having control and a feeling of helplessness over a situation.

Our ego is the human perception of ourselves of this life, therefore, limiting us to our human identity, sense of knowing by interpretation of our environments, or by the people influencing our life. The ego is the voice of negativity or fear that we hear within our thoughts is constantly being fed reasons to keep you in the state of guilt. This overbearing burden to carry the past is a reason to feel bad in your everyday life. Negative voices play in our head saying, "I should have been able to help them," "I shouldn't have put them out" and so forth.

The afterlife focuses on guilt and helps us to cut the cords to it. They use the term "cord" as a means of attachment. The way to release guilt is by allowing yourself personal forgiveness and to free yourself with the truth of what you did or did not have control over. Even if there was a situation that you could have handled differently, it played out the way it did. There were lessons to be learned from the exact way it unfolded. By holding onto guilt, the spirit world looks at it as if we are cramming events into a junk drawer. Every emotion we do not resolve goes into this junk drawer. Again, they want us to cut the cords to the heaviness of guilt and self-punishment.

An exercise I share with my clients who struggle with the acceptance of what is. By breaking down the truth in what you really have control over. When we work with the heart of the truth it makes it difficult to keep feeding the stories to yourself of what you had control over. This can be found in Chapter 14.

You wanted your loved one to forgive themselves for the choices they made. You wanted them to move forward and not judge themselves for the past. Now the healing tables have turned. This is what they unconditionally want from you now. Self-forgiveness is the key to quitting the mind. It offers us a solution to all the inner battles.

Writing Exercise #1

1. Help quiet the mind and focus on one thing at a time. Write down one thing you feel guilty about from this situation.

2. With the aspects you feel guilty about in #1, ask yourself what efforts did you take prior to the final outcome to attempt to help the situation. List all the actions you took.

3. Write down all the things you have control over. Take into consideration, you only have control over your own thoughts and action.

4. Review what you have written and truly digest what you are feeling guilty about. Pay attention to the feelings or sensations you receive in your body or emotions. List your feelings and emotions associated with this piece of guilt.

5. Do you sense any resistance with the idea of letting go of guilt? Holding onto guilt is like white knuckling air because it takes away from your healing process. Breathe through the emotions that arise rather than feeding it with enabling them with negative thoughts. Feelings become blocked when we do not feel through them.

6. Forgive yourself for anything you hold yourself accountable for. Some affirmations to say that can help quiet the mental chatter are:

I forgive myself
I did all I could
They are safe and healed now
It is safe for me to heal
I am forgiven
I trust
I love

Affirmations can help shift the mind to accept a new belief

I partner with the angels in my personal life and in my practice every day. I have personally worked through the punishing feelings of guilt and helplessness with the angels. The techniques I use with myself and my clients is a simple intention, or prayer, to Archangel Michael:

Archangel Michael please dissolve all the cords to
guilt and the heavy burden of self punishment.
I surrender and let go.

This is a modest, but powerful, prayer to ask for divine assistance in the healing process. Remember as your loved ones are not alone, neither are you. Your divine network is waiting for the release of free will to come in a help the healing process.

Forgiveness can be a difficult task to achieve, but it can be your one-way ticket to freedom and peace.
Each time I would work on forgiving someone living or not living, I would end up on the path of sticker bushes, not the promised path to peace. This process was mind boggling, until one day I finished a client session many years ago and I asked the angels why I struggled with forgiveness and letting go. I hope my answer is helpful to you as it has transformed my life.
The angels shared with me that I should talk to the soul when dealing with forgiveness-for myself or in the forgiveness of others. I asked, "Is that the most effective way, speaking to the soul of the person and not needing to speak to the person directly?" The angels have a light sense of humor when they work with me. Their response made me chuckle. The angels said, "Colleen your way is not working out so well, is it?"
As I reflected there was no truer statement. In fact, I was growing irritated and frustrated with my own healing process. So I took the lead of my guides and took them to practice. I sat and envisioned what the soul, or light, might look like. I had a heart-to-heart speaking from my soul to theirs. It made so much sense because the soul is pure and is always alive and listening. Often we get trapped in the thoughts that justify why we should carry

guilt, anger, or resentment. This was freeing because the soul is love and we are not giving a pass on behaviors or the actions of ourselves or others but making peace to breathe forward.

Notes _____

_____

_____

_____

_____

_____

_____

_____

_____

_____

_____

_____

_____

_____

_____

_____

_____

_____

_____

_____

_____

_____

_____

_____

_____

Chapter 9

Communication

If there is one lesson we should discover in life, it would be that communication is key in any relationship. Just like we speak to one another, we can speak to them in the afterlife. Our departed loved ones are always listening and waiting for us to acknowledge them. They love to hear from you and would love for you to talk to them as often as you need or like.

As living beings, communication is vital to having a healthy relationship. The same can be said for the afterlife. They can hear you and feel you at all times. They want us to be able to trust that they are communicating with you back. Souls communicate through a variety of signs. Some of those include symbols, dreams, smells, numbers, birds, or coins. We will go into this more in detail later in this chapter. It is our birthright that we were born with the ability to connect and communicate. It is up to you to fine tune your frequency/vibration to make the connection and trust what you are intuitively receiving. They can hear you and communicate back to you.

To listen to them, we develop our spiritual muscles for Claircognizant. It is the ability to receive information through your thoughts; or clear knowing. Claircognizance is different than a thought. As your abilities to listen in grow, you will be able to tell the difference between your thoughts and the ones they communicate to you. Our loved ones want to strengthen the bond of communication with us. This is not to keep the human connection alive, but to help expand your wisdom of receiving guidance from them now that they are of pure knowledge and have great intelligence and information to share with you.

Some people experience Clairaudience. It is the ability to receive information through listening. Some will clearly hear someone calling their name to try and get your attention or hear whispers to communicate. Often we miss the connection because we think we are making it up. Self-doubt blocks the connection. When we try too hard or have an expectation of what or how we think they should sound, we tend to ignore what is really happening around us and miss the signs.

As you strengthen your vibration and healing, it allows you to build a new relationship with them. Whether you speak aloud or quietly in your head, they are right there listening to you. When speaking with them, be mindful as you talk to them. When you feel as though you could almost hear and feel them, this is them speaking. Feel the way your body responds or how your senses heighten.

Communicating with Me

Your loved ones are more excited to connect and communicate with you, than you are with them. So often when guests come in they have the question, "Is their loved one ok?" Your love ones come through not to let you know that they are ok, but to ease your mind and hearts that you will be ok.

The spirits of our loved ones are always with us. I understand that you want their physical presence to be with you and you miss them, but by having acceptance of the situation at hand, this will help you to establish a new vibrational connection with you. Spirit communication, however, takes some work on their end to relearn how to co-connect with our human vibration, as now the vibration of the afterlife is pure high love frequency. Here on this plane it is much denser. It is up to us here on Earth to strengthen our personal vibration to create a clear airway. When we raise our personal vibration, it opens up to a clearer connection.

As a visual learner, the afterlife has shown me how and why they view grief and vibration:

> Imagine a football stadium. The stands are filled with bleachers along the entire perimeter of the field. You are on the field of life playing the game and your loved ones crossed are up in the bleachers watching you.
>
> When we stop playing the game/living our lives and live in a state of grief our vibration in our bodies becomes lowered, this lowered state has your loved one sitting high up in the bleachers. They can see you but because they are on such high vibration it makes it more difficult for you to receive their signs and messages. However, if you are laughing and doing what brings you joy, even for a moment, your vibration raises and they rush to the sideline of the field as your cheering squad.

Everything is about vibration and tuning into a higher frequency to dial into their station. Like anything else in the world that we are learning, it takes practice and patience but most of all trust.

Signs from the Other Side

Sign...signs everywhere! There are so many ways that the afterlife tries to convey that they are near. Signs from above come in many forms, but the ones below are the most frequently discussed during sessions. This is not to say dismiss signs that you have already established as your loved one. They will be trying to get signs to you in multiple ways.

If you feel you have missed signs in the past, do not worry. Belief is your tool for success when receiving the signs. Spirit is not going to stop giving them; unconditional love and patience are coming through. Many times my clients are lost in the grief that they miss the subtle offerings from the afterlife, but feel elated to know that they have the ability to communicate and connect.

Be open to different signs. I have many clients who try and control the signs they receive. Trying to tell their loved ones what signs they want so they know it is them. This will not bring peace or satisfaction when seeking and receiving signs. Even though your loved ones want you to know you are not alone, the spirit world does not operate on control but unconditional trust. They know we have the ability to connect and want to help us build trust.

My personal goal is to educate you and help you to trust, learn, and connect with your loved one and never to feel dependant on a medium to connect for you. I am a medium and I love connecting you to the messages, but I never want anyone to feel that only mediums have this ability. You have it in you, with some practice, to learn to dial in and up to the other side.

Now let's get to the signs; a direct method of communication. When you see or sense a sign ask yourself, who am I thinking of when it appeared to me? This thought of your loved one is the connection between the physical sign and spiritual connection.

Signs

- Cardinals-The vibrant red coloring is a sign from spirit that is hard to miss. Spirit is trying to get your attention to let you know they are near.

- Blue Jays- The blue jay is a territorial bird that has great loyalty to its nest. When the blue jay makes it appearance to you, know you are being watched and protected. You, the family, and friends are safeguarded.

- Dragonflies- The dragon fly is born underwater. As it matures, it moves its way to a reed or emerging plant where the larva then morphs. It then breaks away from its skin for the adult dragonfly to emerge; hovering over the pond, stream or body of water where it once inhabited. This is a sign from our loved ones that while they are no longer part of our world, they can still watch from above.

- Butterflies-The tranquility and grace of the butterfly is to emerge from one phase of life to another. From the cocoon to caterpillar to the magnificent butterfly- all going with the natural instincts. It is us here that fight the instinctual life cycle. Butterflies are a sign of transcending from this plane to the afterlife (similar to the Dragonfly).

- Ladybugs- Ladybugs are known to be lady luck. When the ladybug lands on you or around you, this is a sign from above asking you to allow joy and fun back into your life.

- Feathers- Feathers are signs from the divine, both angels and loved ones, to say hello with this gentle 'I love you'. Feathers are a sign of freedom, freedom of flight and movement.

- Coins- The saying is, "Pennies from heaven, pay attention." This subtle sign can be found in the most inconspicuous spaces- getting out of your car, on the floor or counter. This is a gesture to just let you know that at all times you are supported.

- Dreams-This powerful sign is very comforting to those who get visitations. If do not dream of your loved one, it does not mean they are not with you. Even though you want them to appear, unconsciously you may block the dream. It might be fear or the reality of their passing. Spirit also can see our healing, and does not want us to stay under the covers to be with them in dream state. If you do not sleep well or are on medication to sleep at night these can affect your dreams as well.
  - Please note: It is never safe to stop medications without the supervision of your physician.

- Suddenly Awake- Waking up in the middle of the night, the hours between 3am and 6am, are often the times you can sense spirit. The soul never sleeps so the physical body and mind are resting the soul can sense the presence of another soul. This typically will happen around the same time each evening or in a window of time. This is a visitation from your loved one.

- Seeing Flashes of Movement- Seeing movement in your peripheral vision is common. Spirit is now light and we can sometimes feel our eyes are playing tricks on us because from the corner of our eyes we catch a flash or a glimpse of something, only to turn around and see nothing with the physical eyes. Do not dismiss this sign or talk yourself out of it. It is a sign!

- Orbs- When captured in a photograph you may see a globe of light surrounding your physical body or in your environment. This is spirit captured on film. It has been frozen within a split second of the photo.

- Smell/Scent- Spirit can also send scent as a sign. If the person was a smoker you may smell cigarette smoke but no one is smoking. The smell of the perfume or aftershave, the smell of their house, a flower that they liked, coffee, food from the kitchen if they cooked or baked, or the smells of someone can take you back into joyful memories of events and times you spent together.

- Music- Upon waking, you may have a song stuck in your head with the chorus repeating itself. Pay attention to what the lyrics say. While driving, a song that the person loved may come on out of nowhere or a song that was connected to a happy time you shared. Music is a key conduit to the afterlife.

- Sensation or Touch- A gentle touch on your cheek or shoulder, the feeling of a hand on your back with the cool sensation that moves from the top of your head through your spine, chills running down your legs or arms are signs of spirit getting your attention. Spirit does not have a physical body so the pressure of the human is not present, be open to the sensations or inner feelings that come through.

- Electronic Activity- The spirits are pure light energy so using electricity to give signs from above is often not missed. Flickering of lights, a call with no number attached on your cell phone, the changing of channels on your TV or car radio can occur. Spirit never wants us to be afraid, so if you are scared to receive than ask Archangel Michael to protect you so that you may feel safe.

- Animals- Animals can sense spirit because they are not driven to listen to their ego. They live by instinct and their natural senses. If your furry friend is acting strange, barking/ wagging their tail or meowing at nothing than it is a good change they are seeing the spirit of your loved ones.

- Buzzing or Ringing In Your Ears- While this may seem bothersome or alarming that something is not right with your ears, it is spirit that sends out tones or frequencies when they are near and trying to get your attention. When you feel this, breathe and ask is there something I need to know? Or think of who you were thinking about when you first noticed the pitch.

Sleep and Dreaming

Spirit is not limited by time, so it is not unusual that they will physically visit between the hours of 3-6 am. The energy of these hours is much quieter during these sleeping hours. During the day, we can become distracted in our own thoughts or everyday life which makes it difficult for us and our loved ones to connect. During the wee hours of early morning, the energy is much calmer and it is easier to feel or sense the subtle realms visiting. Our dreams are one of the avenues that the afterlife uses to visit and communicate with us. It is an area of space and time that are not fueled by ego or hold us back. In a dreaming state, our soul is awakened while our body rests.

There are a few ways to feel spirit around you without seeing them in your dreams. If you notice you are waking up at the same time each night, this is a nudge from heaven to say "I'm here." When falling asleep or waking up in the night, when you spot movement or flashes of light around you, it is not a trick of the eyes. Spirit moving around you might be quick and subtle as to not scare you. Spirit never wants to startle us or make us afraid, so their movements and actions are graceful. In life, we tend to want to force things to happen and in forcing things we become out of balance and can miss the soft gifts from above.

Often I get asked why their loved ones have not come into their dreams. Clients have said that their loved ones have visited family and friends in their dreams but not them. Sometimes, spirit will visit other people to get messages to you. As we have learned, the vibration of grief is very heavy and can block us from receiving their messages. As a loophole to the problem, they will then visit someone else close to you who is not energetically in the same space of grief or despair to get you the loving, comforting message.

Visitation dreams can vary. It might be the person who crossed showing up looking completely healthy and happy, conversing in a way you are used to, or a conversation that is understood by you even though you are not moving your mouths. Spirit can speak telepathically in dreams. So when you wake up and remember a conversation or bits and pieces, know that they were there to help you and be with you. Some spirits might embrace you in a hug or hold your hand, or simply sit or stand next to you.

I am also asked about scary encounters in a dream state. Dreams that are scary, or feel like nightmares, are not visitations. They are fear dreams as thoughts get trapped in your subconscious and show up during sleep state. Spirits do not want to ever frighten you or make you feel more pain.

There are many factors that play into dreaming. Here is an overview:

1. You do not sleep well. If you are waking up a few times a night and not getting a solid night's rest, it makes it difficult for them to come through.

2. The loved ones know that you are hurting and they want you to heal. Clients have made comments along the lines of, "if their loved one visited in their dreams, they would never get out of bed." This is the exact opposite of what your loved one wants for you. They do not want you to forgo your life in the name of them. Therefore, they will not come to you in sleep.

3. Sleep aides and other medications may interfere with remembering your dreams. (If you are on any medications you should NEVER stop them without consulting your healthcare practitioner first.)

4. Each of us receives differently. Be open to all the signs and release getting distracted by just wanting a dream.

Notes _____

_____

_____

_____

_____

_____

_____

_____

_____

_____

_____

_____

_____

_____

_____

_____

_____

_____

_____

_____

Chapter 10

What Now?

As you have read through this book, you have learned about the process of the soul and its journey back home. You have learned that your loved one is safe and always with you. I have also given the beginning steps to establish a communication with your loved ones crossed. All of the information is designed to help ease your mind and answer the questions that have flooded your days and nights. But the elephant in the room still remains; you now belong to a club that no one raises their hand to join and has too many members.

So what now? You still have to grieve and learn to live without the human connection of your loved ones passing and navigate missing them in our daily life. From childhood, we are taught how to build relationships with one another and to give love and nurture the people close to us. We are not taught how to live without the person we loved. Death is the inescapable truth that we all will experience in this lifetime. No one is immune to death. Often the thought of thinking about not having a loved one not being around shakes the heart and we push those feelings away because they are uncomfortable. No two griefs have the same fingerprint because of the unique sacred bonds that we held with that person. People may say they understand, and on some levels they might have a similar experience, but in reality most do not. Everyone is entitled to how they feel.

When will I stop grieving?

Grief has no timeline because each loss is such a personal experience. Grief can feel like waves of emotion that randomly crash on you without warning. Grief can sometimes feel as strong as the love you carried for that person. The angels want you to know how much you are loved. They want to assist you during your times of joy and pain.

Even though you feel powerless over this pain, the angels view it differently. They acknowledge that this grief feels unbearable and that finding your way through it can be messy. The power they do see within you lies in the realm of acceptance.

Acceptance does not mean that you like the situation but that you are willing to see what now reality. By accepting your new reality, it can aid in the process of healing from past traumas you experienced while attempting to save or guide a loved one to get help. Acceptance aids in the navigation of the emotions you encounter throughout the day. Honor those feelings you come a crossed, rather than fearing what is to come in the future. Thinking too far into the future can create fear and resistance in your healing process. Be in your emotions today. Today is your guide and celebrate the moments when you can breathe and not feel pain. These are the powerful baby steps in your healing.

Families will frequently ask their loved ones if the family will grieve forever. Their answer is no. Grief fades over time into missing that person but never releasing the love and the wonderful memories or experiences that you shared with them. You must, however, be willing to be willing at some point in this process to believe that you can reconstruct your life and trust that the angels and loved ones above are right along with you the whole way. Even in death, love and the memories will live forever.

How will I ever be the same?

You will not be the same. Each experience that you have will mold and shape your thoughts and perception of your current reality. This does not mean that you cannot recover from any experience in your life or have joyful moments ever again. It just means you will look at life differently- neither good nor bad, simply different.

When we share the phase "new normal," it is not to be disrespectful of the experience you have had. Instead, it is to help guide you as to why you may be feeling stuck or resistant. They want you to start taking steady steps with each new breath, believing in the days to come without pain or grief.

If your goal is to be the person you were before your loss, than you may feel disappointed as this experience has changed your life forever. The experiences and love you shared with that person has molded your life and well being. Different experiences teach us different things. Therefore, those lessons may make you more sympathetic towards others or situations that you may not have been prior. You may find beauty in someone despite the conditions they are currently in. The angels have always recognized you and your loved ones as beautiful and deserving of love no matter the situation. While the rest of the world may be judgmental and hostile at times, they have a more intimate view.

When you think of your new normal, they encourage you to be willing to remember that your loved one is rooting for you to continue living; not just to get through the day. By taking this into consideration and applying it to your life each day, your new normal becomes filled with compassion and respect for the memories you made. It takes great courage and inner strength to ask yourself, "what now?" and then take deliberate steps to finding out who you are and what you want this next chapter of your life to look like. The angels know that this pain is not your final destination and that you are able to navigate small moments of life, breath by breath. You are being supported as you address your grief and to nurture yourself in the healing process.

Creating a sanctuary or sacred space for you to grieve and honor your loved one may offer you a safe haven to retreat into. Honoring your grief is most important as you are feeling through all your emotions. Your space must be sacred to you; i.e. a bedroom, a favorite chair or space in your vehicle to give yourself the freedom to journal, read, and feel anything uncensored emotionally. This space is your sacred place to host memorabilia, photos and whatever you choose.

Why were my prayers not answered?

The conditions of living in a free will world are much different than the utopian world of the afterlife. They listen and respond to all prayers and intentions that are spoken. While we can put prayer requests in to our angels and God, it is imperative to understand that the one we pray for has to make choices for their own journey as it is still their free will. It is not easy to watch others suffering or struggling when you feel deep down that they are capable of living a different life. The angels are governed by a law of non-intervention. This means they cannot intervene without permission from you as we are equipped with the knowledge and strength to accomplish anything.

When we imagine, or create an expectation, of what life should look like for ourselves and others, we are not always greeted with what we had imagined or expected. This can lead to the feelings that life is not fair or that our prayers were not answered when they do not work out they way we planned them to. It is not that you are being ignored or dismissed. We cannot foresee how situations will turn out or what lessons we need to learn. When we get upset by setbacks or not getting what we had hoped for, this can block our angels from intervening in a helpful way. They have created situations to offer help or blocked you from many situations that you may not be aware of. They do not help us for the praise or acknowledgement. It is their privilege to partner with you. Making choices is a powerful tool. The person making choices holds the power.

Addiction brings the fears of death to the frontline when someone you love is fighting this beast. Addiction can sometimes feel like a battle with the Grim Reaper, and many know and understand the fierce prayers they have directed towards God, praying it was not their loved one. For parents especially, this can be most frightening. As parents, we fret over the risks that life already throws at our children and the choices they will have to make in life in order to lead an independent life. Addiction does not discriminate and our children can be one decision away from this becoming our reality.

As I stated earlier in the book, we do not worship the angels; we partner with them. God sends angels to help us as we send prayers. A difficult lesson I had to learn was praying without attachment. I was always attached to how I thought it should look when asking for resolution to a problem. It only left me to feel let down, unheard, or disappointed. When I learned to pray without attachment, it allowed me to surrender my pain. I had to understand I did not have the whole view of life and I had to allow the best outcome to be presented as the divine was holding my blueprint-the whole picture.

I had to be practical as to what I was asking for and be patient in the process. When your experiencing grief, time feels like a sentence as the waves of emotion rush you without warning. This is the reality of grief. When you love someone so much, grief can often feel equal to the love. The angels want you to know how much you are loved and want to assist you during the times of joy and pain.

Notes _____

_____

_____

_____

_____

_____

_____

_____

_____

_____

_____

_____

_____

_____

_____

_____

_____

_____

_____

_____

_____

_____

Chapter 11

Question and Answer Section

How do you see my loved one?

I see, hear, and sense spirit. When I say *I see*, I am seeing a shadow in the physical world or a flash of light that is moving quickly. The spiritual sight is not only seen through the naked eyes but through the third eye chakra or brow chakra. The third eye chakra is where we have our inner vision or intuitive guidance through spiritual sight. For me, in my third eye chakra, I see the afterlife as an IMAX movie. It is a rather large screen playing movie clips and sharing a multitude of information. Some will have a different experience than mine. When you visually see your loved one within your mind, which is a visitation from them, it is not you just thinking of them and pulling up a memory. This type of visitation can be very comforting for some.

I can also hear them speaking through my thoughts. I tend to hear my own inner voice rather than their voice because it could be overwhelming to hear so many others. I can feel them as energy- not pressure as we feel when the physical body touches us. You may notice a temperature change, cool chill, or a tingling feeling move around your head or hands. As you are learning to strengthen this muscle, keep in mind it takes practice and patience. Do not give up as I have no doubt in my mind that you can do it.

Do they know how much I love them?

They know how much love you them! As spirit, they can see deep within our hearts and can feel the vibration of love. They can hear your words as you talk within your mind and aloud. Spirit now only knows love and is sending you peace love and strength to move into each breath.

How can the other side be better than with me?

Spoken with love from spirit they offer us insight into their world now. It is not to hurt you further or exclude the love and life you shared with them. If situations had been different and they had made a series of different decisions to live healthy, they would have chosen to stay and enjoy the splendor that life offers us. When I speak with spirits they often say that life is beautiful they just had a hard time navigating the journey with the map they were following. Living the addict's life is not joyful or pretty. Many on the other side and in the living have said to me they hated the addiction and they wanted to start fresh. They wish they never got caught up in this web. If they could have beaten the beast, they would have wanted to be with you and share all the moments life had to offer.

Did they purchase a bad batch of drugs?

In the world of street drugs to date, very rarely will the buyer ever buy anything that is pure. The drugs are cut with lethal doses of fillers to create more wealth for the dealers and sellers, with no remorse about this one bit. In answering this question from the messages of spirit to your ears, "There is no good batch of drugs to buy, each pill or bag is a thief of life. It is a game of Russian Roulette and each time we used it was a gamble. The stakes of life were on the table but the inner craving to feed the monster wins most times."

Were they at their funeral?

Yes, I am told by many spirits about the details from their funerals or memorial services. The spirits speak of their view witnessing the eulogy or kind words spoken about them, remembering them for the light, love, and laughter that once filled their lives. They will mention the countless hours of putting picture collages together that were made in their remembrance.

They are so overwhelmed by the turn out of love from family and friends. Often they say that when they lived, they could not recognize the depth of love and concern that people had for them while they had their addiction because they struggled to love themselves and did not feel worthy. The funeral process is for the living as a final goodbye for family and friends. When the soul leaves their body, they start the new journey in the afterlife.

Are they at their graves?

The tradition of graves is for the living. It is a place to share remembrance and respect to someone you loved. The grave is not for the deceased. They have no connection to the sites where their physical vessels lay to rest. The spirit of your loved one is with you always, so if you go to the grave or memorial site, they travel with you. When you get in the car to leave they leave with you.

Many families and friends may feel guilt that they do not go to the graves because it makes it to real that their loved one is no longer here. Many are being cremated and the loved ones living have urns for ashes. I have met with many families who wear cremation jewelry to have the ashes of their loved ones crossed. These acts are all for you in the living state. Your loved one is with you regardless of how or what you choose to do. They attend their funerals to support the people who loved them. They do not feel the sadness of their passing but acknowledge the level of love they really had in this life from everyone.

How should I honor them?

This is a very personal choice and it varies to where and what you feel like you can handle at your stage of grief. You can honor them by starting an organization or scholarship fund in their name to organizing an awareness walk. I have some clients who put their grief into helping others who are still struggling by volunteering or open sober living house. All of these actions can honor your loved ones. Some clients have created healing garden and planted trees in the name of their loved one. Tattoos are often a first thought in remembrance. The real question is how do you want to remember them? What would give you joy and pride in sharing the memory of them with the world?

Do they see the tattoo I/we got for them?

Yes, as we have learned throughout the chapters they are with you and can see the events in your life. The only thing that I hear spirit say about tattooing is they do not want you to brand your body in pain. That means they do not want you to feel pain every time you look at the tattoo. Our bodies are sacred and they want us to heal. It is counterproductive to healing if every time you look at your artwork and feel the pain of their passing. Pick something that gives you joy and peace when you think of them.

**Side note, they are not watching you in the shower or private times, that is your private space and they hold that sacred.

Can they see their child/children they left behind?

Children are the closest thing to God and heaven. They are clear channels to spirits because before they came into this world they were surrounded by spirits. Young children may often express seeing or speaking to a loved one that you may not be able to see. Children are pure and uncensored, as they age they become more influenced by their surroundings and not see and hear as they did when toddlers. We are all born with the gift of intuition. We are capable of this divine connection.

When a soul crosses they are always with their babies/children on the ground offering extra support to them as they grow through the loss of a parent. They often say during their addiction they were not fully present as parents, but now as pure spirit we can live and support them as they deserve.

Chapter 12

Healing Modalities

There does not have to be a ritual, or special invocation, to call on the angels. Simply saying, "Angels help me," is enough. Healing is the language used frequently during my sessions. This can feel foreign in times of confusion or great sadness. The idea of healing does not seem like a concept that can easily be grasped when the heart is feeling such pain. Healing does not mean forgetting the one you loved, but being able to think of them and pain not being your first response.

When we are in the process of healing, we can feel less anxious and breathe full breaths throughout the day. Many people share that the first few months after a loved one's passing that life seems to be a blur. Days feel as they have gone missing and you are trying to make sense of what just happened. You will hear this often from me, or other books on grief, that grief is unpredictable and comes in waves.

There is a vast number of self-help books dedicated to grief on the market, all of which offer different types of explanations and solutions to your healing process. As your grief is unique, so is your healing. Following the passing of their loved one, those surviving might feel protective of themselves and their loved one, especially due to the way they lost them. This can feel like a silent suffocation in order to hide their pain.

As I said before in this book, your loved one had a life prior to addiction. We all came into the world the same way and deserve to be loved, respected and honored. The way your loved one leaves the world is not the legacy they leave in your heart.

I would like to share the healing tools with my clients that are effective but may not be as well known to people who are not familiar with holistic healing practices. I will share with you some traditional practices of grief healing, as well as some that you may not have heard of. These are a gentle introduction to alternative practices, when choosing a practitioner or alternative treatments. I encourage you to research and ask friends, family, or trusted medical professional to help refer you.

All of these modalities are supporting your grief relief as they address your physical body, which has also gone through trauma the same way your emotions have.

Grief Counseling/Psychology Practitioner

Seeking a specialist that has been professionally trained to guide you through grief can be a great partner to you. The process of grief is unpredictable as it comes in waves. When someone passes the people around you may be grieving as well or close friends may not know what to do with your pain. A therapist can offer you a safe haven to grieve and consistently assist you during the traumatic time. Many of my clients have shared that working with a therapist during their immense grief gave them peace, knowing that they were being guided and were able to say everything they felt to an educated neutral party.

Bereavement groups are formed to support and connect with others that are experiencing the emotions of loss. Groups are not for everyone, as it may feel uncomfortable being vulnerable with strangers. Always remember that each person in the room is there because they experienced grief. Whatever stage of healing they may be in, each person in the group has had the discomfort of coming into a situation that is foreign to them.

Validation that you are not going crazy or that others feel the same emotional, physical, and spiritual discomfort as you can be incredible. The journey of grief is very different for each. To many, it feels comforting to know they are not alone.

A group that has a weekly schedule might help to break up the loneliness that comes with grief. Having somewhere to be can help break the cycle of staying home or staying isolated from the world. Sharing coping skills with one another and being able to share your loved one with people. The organizers have been trained to guide the group through steps of healing that can offer optimism as your reconstructing life. You need to be the gauge of where you are in your healing and if any of these choices are right for you at any given time. This may change throughout your grief process.

Reiki

Reiki is an alternative treatment referred often as "energy healing." It comes from the Japanese words "Rei" meaning universal and "Ki" meaning life energy. It emerged in the late 1800's from Japan. Reiki is a very relaxing, non-invasive treatment that focuses on clearing the energy within and the energy fields around your body. Reiki sessions help to heal the emotional and physical body. One way of moving out the stuck, or blocked, energy of emotions is to do energy work. By releasing the backed-up portions of your energy, you help alleviate the mind chatter and allow more fluid energy into your system.

The trained practitioner moves over the body from your head, limbs, and torso with their hands transferring the energy. The trained practitioner may hold a position over the body until they feel a release and feel the flow of energy moving again.

We are all beings of energy with a physical body. When we go through stress, shock, or trauma, the energy over time within our body can get stuck or sluggish; thus causing blockages within our energy. When we have trapped emotions, we can feel this overtime in our physical bodies creating dis-ease. The stuck energy can leave us feeling drained, tired, and possibly ill. As the belief in Chinese medicine that all our emotions are attached to a specific organ, the organs that grief is known to be associated with is the lungs and skin.

While it might be true that I am not an expert in all holistic modalities, it would be remiss of me to not mention that there are numerous options for you to engage in that may help with your grief. I would recommend researching these modalities to see what is suitable to you. Listed below are options available:

- Neuro-Linguistic Programming (NLP)
- Emotional Freedom Techniques (tapping)
- Chakra Clearing
- Acupuncture
- Crystal Healing
- Sound Healing
- Meditation
- Breathing Exercises
- Yoga
- Mediums
- Angel Card Readings
- Massage
- Salt Baths
- Nature
- Exercise

Notes _____

_____

_____

_____

_____

_____

_____

_____

_____

_____

_____

_____

_____

_____

_____

_____

_____

_____

_____

Chapter 13

Trusting Intuition

We are all created equally in the likeness of God which offers us opportunities; a birthright to access intuition. It does not matter how you were raised, your experiences in life, your level of education, or title in your occupation. You are spirit beings doing a human experience. It is our inner GPS that is available to us any time we chose to access it.

I am sure you are wondering, "Well if we have this great tool within us, how come the world seems so screwed up?" Most of us do not know we possess this tool, let alone how to listen to it. When I was developing my intuition many years ago, I questioned why they would not teach this in schools today. This is the most valuable tool I have ever used and apply it every day in every part of my life. In my opinion, the world would be a far more harmonious place if we all connected with the soul. Teaching clients and students to tap into their intuitive abilities is gratifying. By creating the foundation for understanding our intuition, we are able to better connect to the afterlife.

What is intuition?
- Connecting to the language of the soul
- An unwavering source of guidance and direction
- Trusting what you feel, think, and sense

*How do I discern between intuition and
the voice of my inner critic?*

When we learn to calm the mind through breathing, prayer, or meditation, it becomes easier to distinguish between the two. The voice of intuition is always nurturing and consistent in the message it is offering. It is never condemning or harsh no matter what choice you make. It will not coax you into any situations that are not in your highest good.

The voice of ego (your inner critic) is often very confusing and negative. It will bring up times when you struggled or felt unworthy of and support that dialog through your mind.

When you learn to connect with your intuition, this does not mean you will be removed from all uncomfortable human experiences. We still have lessons to learn to help us grow. Connecting with the intuition will help guide us into healthy solutions. Typically when things are hard and you feel like you are constantly battling to get the circle in the square peg, most likely your intuition has spoken to you and through you but that guidance has not been followed. There is no judgment to be made upon you for not realizing that this inner guidance was available. How do you quiet your ego/inner critic?

You do not fight it; you acknowledge it. If you hear streams of negative thinking, than ask your ego to step out. Remember, the voice of intuition will always be loving and gentle. The messages will be repetitive and compassionate. When the intuitive you is speaking internally, if you ask a question for direction you will feel calm and warm inside. We are so programmed to accept negativity that we overlook or dismiss all the positive messages we receive in a day. Whatever we give attention to, the energy flows in that direction. When we are sad or grieving it is hard to see the positive or light in our world.

When connecting into your intuition remember this: you are in control. The ego evokes thoughts of guilt, shame, fear, or pain. These messages play through your mind as mental war plays out. The ego often starts message with the word "YOU." It uses phrases like, "You should have done" or "You could have."

When we are being guided by intuition, it does not start with the words YOU. We are free will beings and our intuitive-self knows this. Often the messages are missed because they come through as ideas or feelings. For example, your intuition may suggest "Call Mary." In calling Mary, she may have information or a connection to a concern that you have. You may hear "slow down" while driving and after acknowledging it, find that you avoided an accident. The possibilities are endless as to what life situations intuition can guide you through.

How do you receive?

Intuitive information can come in many forms: images, symbolic pictures, vivid dreams, verbally hearing words in your mind, or through your thoughts. Our intuition is always on but it is up to us to recognize them and make the choice to take action.

It is an inside job

As cliché as it may sound, listening to your gut or following your heart holds great value in building your intuition. It has been referred to as "following a hunch," "going on instinct," or "listening to your gut." Whatever you call it, the reality is that it is your first sense. Not everyone is born with all five senses working as they should. Everyone, however, is born with intuition.

As we spoke in the previous chapters, raising our vibration is essential in feeling, sensing, and connecting with our intuition and our loved ones in the afterlife.

Tuning into the Souls Station

Connecting with spirit can seem foreign and confusing in the beginning because we are embodied with numerous emotions. To help you understand the visual aspects of connecting, I invite you to think of the afterlife as a radio station.

A radio offers many channels of listening enjoyment. If you wanted to listen to Jazz, you would adjust the dial to tune into a specific Jazz station. Sometimes, adjusting to a specific station might not work for where you are. It is not to say music is not playing on that station at all; it very well may. But it does not work for where you are or what is going on around you. It can leave you feeling frustrated and defeated if it does not work properly. But this just means you need to find another station that works for where you are.

Often times when we struggle with a station, it is because emotionally we are not aligned or ready to connect. Finding alignment is essential to connection. When we are not in alignment with the higher vibrations, we are not compatible with their unwavering station. We must align emotionally to their station. Healing is needed in order to build a higher vibration and connect with those we love.

Chapter 14

Healing On Purpose

I have provided a course that you can work through at your own pace to help relieve some of your pain and anguish. This course was designed by the angels to help you learn to heal and release emotions that surface. This course should not be taken until you are willing and ready to make small, yet significant, shifts in your ways of thinking and living. Please note that I have skipped the notes pages for this chapter because most clients who have done this before felt it was best to use a journal to continue the practice. If you feel you only want to try this a couple times just to experiment with your feelings and where you are now, feel free to use a couple sheets of paper at a time and discard them after. Take your time and be honest with yourself.

The steps to help release pain and pent up emotions were first given to me during a dark period of my life. When the angels taught me these steps, I was laying on the bathroom floor in emotional agony, asking "Why is everything I know and love being stripped from me?" After putting my children to bed, I would retreat to a space I felt safe enough to curl up and allow myself to feel something other than helplessness and fear. In the confines of my head, I would constantly raise the question "Why me?" Having an adult spiritual tantrum would only aggravate me because I knew I was a good person and only wanted to help people but life was not being fair to me.

As I laid on the floor sobbing, a clear voice spoke to me in my head. Archangel Michael told me to get up and look at myself in the mirror. He was gentle, yet assertive. I did as I was bid, but I hardly recognized myself. I looked shattered. My makeup had been flooded by tears making it cascade down my face. The voice came in with strength again, asking me what I saw. I responded, "A failure and heartbroken woman."

He said, "We see a fighter. Only the fighter we see has yet to fight for herself. She has compromised herself and given her power away and fought like a heavyweight boxer for everyone she loved but her."

I acknowledged he was right. I had surrendered myself in the name of everyone and everything else. Who was this woman in the mirror who owned many masks to show up to the roles that were expected of her? Who was I? He was there telling me God had not rejected me. Instead, he was protecting me from further harm. I had been resisting my inner voice that said I was dying inside and living in the shadows of hope that things would change was only taking me away from the things the life I had stored secretly deep in my heart and only shared with God during my prayers. To speak my desired life aloud would only cause more pain inside of me and distract me from my roles in life. If I said out loud that I wanted a different way, a different life, I knew that I would have to make changes and I was afraid of what life looked like outside of my reality.

That day changed my whole life direction. I went to bed drying my tears all while feeling the heaviness of my chest lessen and my breath become more harmonized to find a rhythm. I closed my eyes for the first time in months without an ache in my heart.

As I fell asleep, the angel whispered, "Tomorrow, I will teach you the steps to heal and one day after you have mastered this part you will teach it to others." In the state I was in, I snickered at the idea of life feeling any different than that moment. I was exhausted simply wanting to think of nothing more and enjoy this moment of peace.

Well, here I am as my own testimony to these life saving tools. I say life saving because this awareness has changed, shifted, and upgraded my life to levels I did not know were possible. I have a great respect and compassion for wherever you are on your journey to finding yourself. I also know the gentle steps that we need to commit to ourselves. These patterns did not show up overnight and they will not just go away overnight. Patience in healing is a gift because it allows us to feel confident in the steps left behind us and optimistic to the steps before us. With each progressive step, you will feel more confident with your ability to target the source of what is not working for you which will help release the symptoms of discomfort in your life.

> The Japanese have an art form called *Kintsukuroi*, meaning golden repair. This art form is centuries old where they take broken pottery and mold it with a special lacquer with powdered gold, silver, or platinum. By taking a broken object and molding it with precious metals, such as gold, it brings value and purpose back to that object. Your golden lacquer is your new knowledge that helps fix you and help align yourself for the better.

You are not broken or irreparable. When moving into feeling exposed, the pieces that were hiding you broke away like a shell that had many fractures. Your true self is a divine light being. You are powerful and capable of starting a beautiful relationship with yourself. Are you ready?

In this next segment, your course will begin. There are four parts and multiple questions and things to consider. These four parts that you will learn will become your master tools to navigate through any situation.

Information is power and to empower yourself we are taking the first steps into the emotional investigation. Give yourself time each day to go through the questions and keep your answers as we will revisit them in step two. There is no need to rush through it as you can go at your own pace. Keep a journal in a safe, private space so you find it comfortable to be 100% honest with yourself. Information is power. The more mind-blowing realizations that you will have about yourself, the more you will start to feel empowered about your future and trust the intuitive part of you to move forward with confidence!

Acknowledge

1. What areas in your life do you feel resistance to?

2. How long have you been feeling this resistance? Are you ignoring thinking about it or ignoring the discomfort?

3. Be aware and take mental notes to the flow of subtle negative thoughts and beliefs that repeat each day surrounding this situation.

4. When you are thinking of making changes or upgrades to your life, how much fear is presenting itself? You can list

this on a scale from 1 to 10 (1 being the least amount of fear and 10 being the most).

5. How do you feel this fear? (Example: Does it feel more like a road block or a danger in your life?)

6. What emotions show up? (i.e. guilt, fear, sadness, frustration, anger, etc.)

7. How often do you create "the worst case scenario" when thinking about a change?

8. Do you attempt to control other people's lives rather than pay attention to your own journey?

9. When looking to change, do you always think of other people's happiness before your own? Do you worry about what others think of you?

10. Do you feel your personal happiness is selfish?

11. Do you blame a situation, or person, for your inability to find happiness or grow?

12. How often do you tell stories of your hardships or situations that you are unhappy with?

13. Do you feel worthy of happiness, joy, or fulfillment in your life?

14. Does self doubt, based on past experiences, keep you stuck?

15. Due to the fear of failure, how paralyzing does it feel when you are looking to try something new?

16. How often do you ask others their opinions of what to do?

17. Do you identify yourself by the opinions of others?

18. How do you identify yourself?

19. How often is the sentence, "I am," followed by something negative?

20. Are you afraid of being vulnerable?

21. Is vulnerability seen as a weakness or strength when making changes?

22. What physical symptoms do you feel with your physical self?

23. Do you hide from situations that make you feel uncomfortable?

24. Do you overreact or argumentatively defend yourself?

Now that you acknowledge what the issues are and where you are finding yourself struggling, how do you progress in your healing? Taking an ownership of why you feel a certain way is equally important. If it is your thoughts, actions, or choices than you should own it- the good, the bad, and messy.

In this section, it is a judgment free zone. It will be easy to start punishment and persecution thinking; however, this is where you must exercise great power that you have within you. I would say an affirmation to myself, "I did what I knew how to do. I am learning a different way now." This affirmation helped me to reset the momentum towards growth and push the stop button on the old tapes of a mental beat down. We have no control of outside forces that bleed into our life; however, it is our sacred duty to ourselves as to how we respond. When we feel broken or unheard, we become immune to the idea that we have a say in anything. Situations that you currently, or previously, lived may have been your normal but we are creating a new normal now. Small deliberate steps create life changing movements towards your dreams of a happy emotionally healthy life!

Ownership

1. Do you feel a situation has you trapped?

2. Are you left wondering how did I get here or why am I here again?

3. Do you notice a recurring pattern of situations and people in your life?

4. Do you have or did have a choice in your situation? If in an unhealthy marriage, do you say I do not have a choice; I don't have money, resources, anywhere to go? The truth is we always have a choice but may not like the options. Full ownership is a choice.

5. Do you harbor resentment for other people disrespecting you?

6. Do you tell the same stories of your unfortunate events to people or whoever has an ear?

7. Do you hold yourself hostage as a victim of someone else's poor behaviors and actions?

8. Do you stay in unhealthy situations, family, work relationships in the name of love?

9. Do you make future plans for yourself and sacrifice today?

10. Does the feelings of not wanting others to judge or criticize you keep you feeling trapped?

11. Do you worry about what others think of you?

12. Do you use your voice and say what you want?

13. Do you know what you want?

14. Do you have unhealthy coping mechanisms? Drinking, self medication, overeating, or shopping in excess?

15. Do you find yourself comparing your life to others?

16. Do you feel unworthy of happiness and joy?

17. Is fear holding you back?

18. Are you afraid of losing people if you change?

19. Did you learn from adults or family members you respected to just give and not receive?

20. Do you dream of a different way of living?

21. Would a different way cause you to do something unfamiliar? Go back to work, change jobs or change your lifestyle?

22. Is your lifestyle or the comforts of it holding you hostage?

23. What words do you speak most often out loud about yourself? Negative self talk or self deprecating even if in a joking matter?

24. Do you feel obligated to "sleep in the bed you have made" and now you are stuck in it?

25. How much time a day do you dedicate to yourself?

26. How often do you spend in past thinking? "If I had done this" or "if I did not do that".

27. How easily do you forgive others?

28. What boundaries do you have in your life?

29. Do you feel respected or validated by people in your life?

30. Do you believe people know you or what you allow them to see?

31. Will you shy away from things that you feel you will fail at?

The words "let go" and "release" can cause the mind to go into overdrive and the body seize up with tension and confusion. When we are in the discovery phase of the first two principles, you allowed your heart and soul to be expansive and curious as to what comes up. The release phase aligns the energy with your discoveries and awareness and becomes easier to digest and graceful to execute.

Now what? How do I let go? I have designed this next piece with options and choices to see what fits for you at this juncture of your journey. You may choose to utilize all the techniques of feel drawn to one.

Release

1. Create a Release Box:

    This can be something you create or any container that has a lid. Write down on a piece of paper what you feel and deposit the pieces of paper with what you want to release into this container. Take this opportunity to surrender fear, doubts, and the unknown. Fill the box with all of your worries as you have carried them long enough. Now you seek solutions, guidance, and direction.

    The constant action of writing down what you are worried about will become evident as to how unconsciously we are focused on our situation and not the resolution. The more you write it out and release those pent up emotions, you will become mentally more aware of the direction of your energy. The law of attraction, where your thoughts go energy flows.

    I made a mine and called it a God Box. This was a huge partner to me while doing this exercise. I am an action person, so just writing it out I was letting something go that did not satisfy me as a release. This led to my building trust in the process.

2. Trust:

    Trust that when you ask God, the angels, and the universe to take away all of your worries, they have received your request. What blocks this from fully releasing is our desire to keep holding onto it or not seeing the desired outcome before we let go. This is counterproductive to the process.

You must let the old energy out to bring in the new. That is why you spent so much time investigating what is not aligned. When you are asking for a release, trust that the angels only want the highest outcome for you, so they will rush to your side to assist, as we are a free will world, which mean the angels and the universe and the divine cannot interfere or remove something our free will is holding on to.

One day, the angels asked me why I prayed for the same situation to be resolved day in and day out? Thinking it was an odd question, I replied simply, "Because I want help." They said, "We see this and need you to stop blocking the help. Every time you think of your worries and repeat your request, you are pulling it back from us." This was very eye opening to me, as I learned I was praying for help but taking it back the request by continuously asking. Praying is a form of relaxation to my worried mind, but I was not in a space of trust but fear of the unknown.

If this sounds like you, this next exercise might be helpful. Buy latex balloons (only if you do not have sensitivity to latex) and then write each of your requests on them. In an indoor/inside (as balloons are harmful to wildlife and environment) location hold the string of the balloon in your hand and then let them go, trust that your team in the invisible realms has the request and are on it. Now you must have patience and without attachment to how the outcome should look so that the best outcome can be delivered. Often we pray for specific outcomes based off our wants in the current situation, but not everything we want is good for us emotional, mentally, or physically. Miracles need room to grow, so give space to the situation.

3. Journaling:

This is a great release tool as this allows a free space for you to think and be open and honest with your intentions. Often when we write we can feel within us if we are lying to ourselves. This is your space so be open and honest with yourself.

4. Cutting etheric cords:

Cutting cords to people and situations can be helpful when releasing pent up energy. We are energy and we exchange energy with every person and situation you are in or have been in. Cords are energetic connectors that allow a flow of energy to pass through. When we ask Archangel Michael to please dissolve the cords attached to people, we are freeing ourselves from feeling the emotions and energy of others.

In society, we think connection is good but we do not necessarily see it as an energetic connection. These can leave us in a low vibrational drained space when we do not detach. It is called *Detaching With Love*. This technique is so powerful as it allows you to be in charge of your actions and energy.

We can always ask for help:

*Archangel Michael, Please dissolve all cords
to fear, pain, worry, relationships, family
experiences from the past that are creating
unhealthy feelings and behaviors.*

Depending how thick the cords are, you may have to repeat this numerous times to fully feel the release.

5. Chanting, Singing or Dancing:

These can raise your vibration and can help move out dense or stuck energy. The old energy is stuck or dense so it moves sluggishly. These will help to push through the dense energy more efficiently and in a fun, uplifting way.

6. Breathing:

Imagine taking deep healing breaths and with that inward breath you are gathering all the emotional clutter that you have uncovered. Exhale and let go of everything. This can be a great starter tool as breathing is the tool that is always available to us. Centered breathing helps to ground our energy and to create a moment of silence within you. Notice your physical body when you do this. Feel your shoulders drop and your jaw loosen into a subtle shift of relaxation.

Visit my website to download a free beginners breathing meditation.
www.ColleenStMichaels.com

7. Exercise/Yoga:

Exercise in any manner is a release of energetic blockages and it releases happy endorphins into our system. It helps to manage and control the stress and anxiety within you.

8. Choices to Grow:

Hold sacred your choices to grow. Give yourself permission to withhold yourself from surrounding yourself with people or situations that may feel unsupportive or toxic.

9. Nature:
     Spending time in nature is a life support tool. Nature consists of pure and high vibrations that help you release build up naturally. Walking barefoot on the ground below you can help calm and reset your energy. The ocean is always moving, so standing in front of the ocean imagining giving all your worries and concerns to the ocean as it moves out it takes the release with it. The water moves in replenishing you with pure energy.

10. Bath Soak or Epsom Salt:
     Baths help to detoxify the system and soothe the muscles. Our bodies are recording devices of life, any pain, shock, or trauma that you may experience is held within the body, muscles and cells. The release goes much deeper than "I do not want to think about this anymore". It is being released from your cellular memory.

The exercises for Raw Writing in the next chapter can also be a valuable tool when releasing. Check it out in the next chapter.

Rebuilding

   This is your life by design now! You have created the space to receive all the new into your life. What do you want?
   Write a list of what you want and then affirm I am worthy, we will always be deconstruction as long as we are breathing. This reconstruction of life is exciting and is filled with wonderful experiences and miracle ready for you to claim.
   When we are rebuilding we don't just sit and wait for life to come to us, we set our intentions and then let it go. When the seed is planted we cannot see it under the earth but we still nurture and water the seed with expectancy of its arrival into a

plant. The same goes for this, plant the seed, water, and nurture yourself as it goes through the phases of life and enjoy the harvest.

Chapter 15

Developing the Medium's Muscle

Developing the medium's muscle is a process of receiving, trusting, and believing.

Like any strong connections in the physical world, you have to be open to communication and the process of giving and receiving. The same applies to the afterlife; they want us to know that they are with us and that we have the built in connection right within us. Logic does not prevail in the process of building in your spiritual muscle; ego can feed logic and dismiss what is being received. Trust in the invisible realms that with proper preparation of protection you will feel safe and confident.

Many have not been taught that this is okay. However, many have been taught to fear it or hide it, so they are not shunned or made fun of. Over time of blocking communication, eventually, you turn the dial so far away from you that it is hard to hear.

The foundation of any spiritual practice is to TRUST, BELIEVE, AND PRACTICE. In this segment of the book, we will learn the safest and most effective way to connect with spirit

Everyday things that can block receptivity

Attachment - This can confuse or block the connection because we might dismiss the message from how we knew the personality of the person before they crossed. Remember, the free will of the person is when they were living. Anything not attached to love does not cross. Release attachments of what you think they would say and be open to their new view through their view.

Expectations- Setting expectations in life can be disappointing. Same goes for the afterlife. We do not understand what they are experiencing so setting expectations from our human interpretation will lead to disappointment or the feelings of sadness thinking our loved one or person crossed isn't listening. They are all knowing now so they know who we are and our capabilities. They want us to stretch into trust a little further and allow their communication to come through.

Grief- Grief can lower your vibration and create an energetic distance in the reception.

Acceptance- It is critical when you have not accepted a person passing. I will be difficult to believe or acknowledge they are not here, making it a blockage for communication.
Acceptance does not mean embracing it; it means that you acknowledge the truth in it.

Alcohol or Substances- They can interfere with the receptivity of receiving because it lowers the human vibration. We are looking for clear communication and that means a clear channel to move through.

Dismissing or Missing Signs- The human ego can be sly when it chooses. Asking spirit to give us a sign that they are near is a divine gift from them when received. It is our job to be open and trust that it is them.

Feeling Grounded- If you feel the days are sweeping past you and you feel disconnected or out of focus, then that is a sign of not being grounded. When we are disconnected from the physical world or spending too much time in our heads, we are then overlooking the precious gifts from our loved ones crossed.

Fear- When you are afraid you naturally are blocking because fear lowers our vibration and kicks our ego into control. With the proper angelic partners with you, you can go safely into the afterlife.

Releasing Negativity

Drama filled life or living within a negative mindset- Negativity is a lower vibration and it is fed by the ego. We live in a society where negativity is welcome, be mindful of your beliefs and thoughts to check in and shift out the negativity. Your goal is to connect with the highest vibration to have a clear connection. Drama is never a pathway to clarity.

The spirit world wants us to feel peace in knowing they are ok and peaceful. We muddle the process with human self-doubt and disbelief. It is easier than we feel it should be.

Steps to connection

Find yourself a quiet space alone where you can set aside at least 15 min to start.

1. Take 3 deep breaths
    *   Breathe deep from your lower belly and then push the air out through your mouth. After the second breath, feel your body become less tense and feel your shoulders drop as you move in to the last breath.
    *   There is a meditation on my website for this.

2. Ask Archangel Michael or the light of God to shield and protect you
    *   This step is non-negotiable. We must have a deep respect as you are going into an unfamiliar area. This not to scare you. As there is light present, there is also darkness. In shielding yourself with divine light, it offers you protection from tricksters or negative spirits. I view this protection as if I were entering an elevator. If I wanted to go from ground level to the third floor, I would press the 3rd floor button. It would take me to my destination without question. Same as connecting in with the higher vibrations of the afterlife.

3. Affirm that you receive in trust, "I Trust"
    *   Affirmations create a new stream of thoughts or patterns within you, the more you say it the more it becomes your reality.

4. Ask the EGO to step out. Remember your ego wants to confuse you or put you down.
    *   The simple phase EGO OUT

- The ego is not your amigo

5. Ask or Write down the person you wish to connect with
   - I prefer to write and I teach my students to use pen and paper, I have felt it helps to silence the mind by redirecting your thoughts to writing.
   - Some sample questions to ask
     - What do you want me to know?
     - What signs do you give?
     - Are you with me?
   - You can ask general questions to start, you may get one or sentences. You will hear it come through your own thoughts and in your inside voice. If the messages are confusing or negative this is your ego, set your ego aside again and try again.
   - Spirit speaks with love and patience; it does not put us down or judge.

6. Ask questions and then write what you receive. Do not dismiss the messages.
   - Write whatever comes up.

Feel free to practice this as often as you can. Practice strengthens the muscle and develops trust.

Remember, this gift is already inside you. We are working to release the doubt and raise your vibration. Keeping your vibration high is key. If you are in a bad space, this is not the time to connect.

Ways to raise your vibration:
- Listen to music
- Take a walk
- Journal

- Trust
- Healthy foods
- Faith
- Meditation
- Practice relaxed Breathing
- Crystals to help calm your energy

Ask friends or family if you can practice with them. Say whatever you receive. Be mindful if you feel judgment or an opinion it is your EGO that is speaking. Spirit does not judge us or criticize us. Reset yourself, put ego out, and start again.
Journal your daily exercises, looking back you can see how far you have come.

Remember to ask questions. ASK! We are developing a line of communication.

Pay attention to the signs that you are getting from the afterlife:
- Ringing of the ears
- Finding feathers
- Being woken up in the early morning hours (3-6am)
- Feeling temperature changes
- Seeing flashes of colors or in your peripheral vision catching something in the corner of your eyes with your spiritual sight-*Clairvoyance- you can learn more about your Clairs in my meeting Clair online class on my website*
- Acknowledging that when you think of a person that you want to connect with that this is them near you
- Dream visitations
- Feeling a tingle on the top of your head
- Placing your hands out and closing your eyes and ask them to touch your hands
- Sensing or feeling an energy around you-*Clairstience-you can learn more about your Clairs in my, Meeting Clair online class*

- Listen to your own intuition

This is a sacred connection, to be respected and treated with love.

Writing Raw

This is a release exercise, when we release in a healthy way what we have been holding inside we create more space to heal and grow. Often we are not taught to feel anger, frustration, jealousy and the not so pretty feelings, but yet we have them. When these emotions boil over it usually leads to outburst of anger or misdirected rage. Writing raw has been my greatest tool in moving through my emotions.

1. Get paper and pen.
2. Write anything and anything that comes to your mind.
3. Vomit on the pages (screw proper English and punctuation. Hell, screw writing neatly on the lines). Write all the bottled up feelings and let them fly onto the page.
4. Allow crying and just write.
5. Do not reread what you just wrote, it serves no purpose.
6. Rip it up, shred it, or dispose of it, so no one ever see it.
7. Breathe and exhale.

Repeat this as often as you need, this exercise gives you the freedom to say and think whatever you like. I use it for everything now, if I get angry, I write. If I get jealous, frustrated, or anxious, I write. I have learned that I am often not upset at the situation in front of me but all the bottled up emotions that I never let myself feel in the past.

Meditation

On my website, I have free downloads that will guide you through a variety of meditations. Feel free to use it as you start your journey in finding peace in a new normal.

Meditation has many benefits, improves memory, connection with spirit, clarity, body function, reduces stress, allows access to self awareness, focus and more, but the name alone can feel very intimidating when your mind is so busy. The thought of being still seems impossible. My mind has always been busy and I was frustrated as I started into my journey of meditation. I would go to meditations at different healing centers hoping to reach that Zen zone everyone raved about, but all I could do was lay there with the list of crazy that were flying through my head. At the end when everyone was sharing, I felt envious of their ability to take journeys and see magical things. Needless to say, I left feeling pissed and discouraged. I did not give up. Soon, I realized that I would have to find a way that I could feel successful with it. Breathing! My "ah-ha" moment came and I could breath and feel relaxed. So I started to set my timer for 5 minutes (anything more than 5 minutes I would have quit). Set a timer based off of where you are and then started with a deep breath in and then a loud exhale. The loud exhale became a guide that distracted me from thinking of everything in my head. This was how I started and was able to teach my students who felt just like I did. Many years later, I have evolved into a successful meditation practice and to this day start all my personal meditations like this.

Feeling and sensing spirit

You are a spirit being having a human experience. We are remembering something that is already in us. Let the love in your heart guide you.

The essence of spirit is light and peaceful vibration, so when we are learning to tune into the subtle realms of energy we must know what we are looking for. This practice is new to many so we may want to feel the physical touch that we experienced when they were living. Again it is the subtle realms, so we must learn to become peaceful and free of expectations when we are practicing these techniques. In this exercise we are going to explore the sense of feeling our loved ones crossed by sensation. As all of the practices that we go over, patience and trust is the confidence builder.

1. Find a quiet space where you can be alone.
2. If you chose, light a white candle- white candles represent purity.
3. Ask Archangel Michael or the light of God to surround you.
4. Close your eyes.
5. Take a deep breath and exhale (remember to breathe during this entire process). I know that sounds silly but often in anticipation people hold their breath. Breath is balance giving and receiving
6. Put your hand out in front of you, palms up.

7. Ask insert name to let you feel them.

8. Pay attention to any temperature or pressure changes around your extremities or head.

    1. Do you notice a coolness moving side to side?

    2. Do you notice any tingling on your fingertips or at the crown of your head?

    3. Do you feel your body getting a chill or shivers?

Living with Compassion

I do not know what stage of life you are living. I hope the information has helped you on some level. If just one piece of information resonates with you at this moment, then I feel joy for you. Be gentle and have great compassion for what you are feeling. Never mind where anyone else wants or believes you should be. This is your journey and I hope you feel supported, loved, and nurtured by your divine team.

Living life without the one you wanted to live it with is not an easy process, be gentle and have compassion for yourself as you take one breath at a time. In the depths of pain it's hard to see yourself. You are in control of your thoughts, feelings, and emotions. Your loving team of divine support is with you each step of the way cheering you along. In the end when it is your time to cross, they will be there with outstretched arms and love.

Chapter 16

Stories

Over the years, I have been blessed with meeting so many beautiful people in my line of work. I am truly grateful to have grown personally with the stories they have shared. I find great inspiration from people living in unthinkable situations and how they have found grace in their chaos. With you now, I would like to share some of these stories with you so you can possibly find comfort.

For privacy reasons, names and specifics have been changed out of respect. Nevertheless, I hope you find comfort in their stories.

I'm Safe

I stepped out of my office door to greet my next guest in the waiting room. Considering I shared an office space with multiple therapists at that time, I was never certain as to who my next client would be. When I looked at the few people waiting, I noticed a woman on the sofa with her shoulders rounded over with weak and exhausted energy around her.

After our initial greeting, I walked her through an explanation of how my sessions normally flowed as a medium. I shared information about the afterlife and dispelled myths that were normally questioned. I asked specifically that she not provide me information, as I like to establish a connection organically and then she could proceed to ask me whatever she would like.

Within minutes into our session, I was connecting with a young male who passed from an overdosed. Her body instantly trembled, with tears flowing freely down her cheeks. She cried out, "That's my son."

His first words to her were, "Mom, I am safe and I am sorry. I didn't see when I was struggling how you were equally struggling too. You had a different drug than I did. Your drug was the love of me. You have to know I am safe." She expressed that on her way to the office for this session, in the car, she spoke out loud to him asking for him to just say he was "safe".

We went through the rest of the session with her asking questions she had been punishing herself with. As we came to an end, she shared with me the inside view of her long fight side by side with her son. The addiction occupied her every waking moment. Year after year of hoping for recovery to stick with him and then the spirals of relapse, only to finally face the harsh reality that he only had two options: Recovery or Death. The idea of having to come to terms with such a reality was more than she could comprehend but could no longer avoid. She expressed to me that her fears become reality as she got the news of her child's passing as she said, "death won."

Even though I work with the afterlife every day, my heart went out to this woman. I felt heavy with compassion and love for her. As a fellow human being and mother, I wanted her to know she was safe and supported. I held the space for her to just be in her words and in the emotion of what she said. I wanted her to find the next breath in an environment that was safe for her to sob and feel safe in without having to hold back. She had held her own grief in order to support her family as they moved through their own stages of grief.

Once she started to catch her breath, I simply asked her, "How can I support you?" With a mixture of surprise and confusion, she sat there perplexed at my question. I continued with, "I have connected and delivered the messages that I was given from your child and the angels that are supporting you. You expressed you felt relief from knowing they were safe and felt validated in our connection that it was indeed your child. So now, how can I support you?"

She expressed that she came here to find peace but the question of how I could support her threw her off. No one had ever asked *how* they could support her and she frankly did not know how she needed to be supported, just that she needed it. She continued to explain how she knew everyone meant well but they would constantly use expressions to "relieve me" of grief. She understood everyone meant well but it was something she did not believe and did not want to hear.

Her response to not wanting to be rude to people attempting to show sympathy or to avoid anyone with her day-to-day feelings, she let the calls go to voicemail and ignored those around her. She felt guilty to admit that she resented those who still had their loved ones and made comments like, "their better off" or "you can move on now." Without her consciously accepting it, she allowed herself to grieve in silence and to live in pain forever. She said, "I believed I could wear this mask for the world to see so I could get through my day. I could cry in my car when no one was looking and it would be fine."

I came to find out that the only reason she scheduled an appointment with me was because a friend had suggested it to her. She felt silly, and skeptical, for even agreeing to it. She had already admitted to feeling so broken inside from this experience, but honestly, what did she have to lose at this point? As she turned to leave the office, she asked for a hug which I readily gave. Hugs can say things words cannot seem to express sometimes.

Upon leaving she acknowledged I could still help support her. She now wanted to learn and to grow. She wanted to fully cope with her grief and acknowledge the pain head on. She did not want to feel dead inside any longer.

I often meet people in this stage of grief. I feel grateful they show up and are willing to explore a different road to healing. That is what she received. This woman found a different road to healing. She later told me that after her session she started to notice the signs of her son around her. She was able to laugh again and feel life rushing back in through her veins. It had been absent for so long, but now it was back. It had been a very long time since she could enjoy life and do things she had once enjoyed without feeling guilty or in line with the "grieving mother" stigma.

The irony of the situation is all she wanted was for her son to get better and to change his ways. She wanted him to break free from this disease and to stop hurting. She had told him he was strong enough to do it; he needed to. Now that's all her son wanted for her. He wanted her to find peace. It was now up to her to decide if or how she wanted to heal. She was introduced to both the holistic world and to mainstream modalities. She had risen above her grief. Since then, she has stepped out of the darkness and into the light.

In my line of work, I have two teams in the invisible reams that I work alongside: Angels and our loved ones crossed. As an angel intuitive and spiritual medium, I have access to a world many may not understand.

Although I explained it earlier in the book, I would like to revisit some key pieces of information. Angels have never walked the earth, but are sent to watch over us and guide us through life through our intuition. Our intuition is our soul's GPS through life to help guide us toward fulfilling our life purpose here on earth. The angels speak through our intuition, inner thoughts, or sensation in our physical body. The angels have immense compassion and understanding for us at all times. They know who we are on the soul level and why we are here doing this earth walk. They are restricted to entering into our path without invitation by free will. It must be us who allows the divine assistance to come into our lives by asking.

In sessions, not only do I deliver the messages from our loved ones crossed but the sacred messages from our beloved team of angels. The angels and our loved ones share space in the divine . and offer us tools to healing through this unthinkable grief. We always have angels around us. When we are struggling and in times of great pain and sorrow, we have so many more waiting for us to allow them in to ease the ache, create comfort, and offer support.

In this next story, I would like to share one woman's experience with gaining insight. This mom's story is one of the many clients I have sat with over the years who suffered with the loss of her daughter.

Another Mother's Story

Awareness is the first word that comes to mind when I think back on my journey of my daughter's passing. I now realize this was always in me and my soul always knew deep down. I was put on this path and I do believe, with the help of my daughter from another plane, signs immediately started to come in. I was so grateful. I continue to be open to signs now.

For me, it is now easy for me to follow the leads from my angels. Like most people, I was not the praying type and I hardly paid attention to signs. My grief was severely painful. For anyone who has lost a child or loved one, I am sure some of you can relate.

One random day, I got a phone call from my stepdaughter telling me her sister had been attempting to get her attention from the other side. She left work without understanding what was wrong. To save a long story, we ended up at Colleen's office shortly after. This office visit was nothing short of life changing for me. It opened my heart, mind, and soul.

My daughter, who had passed, had been trying to get our attention. She had been trying to communicate with us. In the two hours we were there, she pointed me in the right direction for my healing. My story with my daughter is personal but what she opened my eyes to was nothing short of beautiful. I am now awake; pointed in the right direction of healing. I knew I had my angels; I knew my daughter, mom-mom, and dad were with me and ok. I no longer feel alone or have fears of death. I am worthy of love and guidance.

People ask how my daughter's passing can lead me to feeling inner peace, elation, and love. Her love gave me love. The feeling is incredible. I was so lost before I realized I had a team of angels to support me.

Since then, I have learned so much about life, the afterlife and myself. I have met amazing people that I have been lead to. Before I purchase books I pray and ask the angels to help pick the ones that will most benefit me to learn more and literally books fall in my path. Every book I've read has been amazing!

I was so thirsty for knowledge. Now, I read everything! Where I never prayed before, I now find myself praying. I feared God wasn't listening but I know now He is. How can my daughter's passing lead me to feeling inner peace, elation, and love? While I miss my child more than anything in the world, my soul was healed. I'm still learning still reading just can't get enough. To think it all started with a sign and an Earth Angel, Colleen St. Michaels.

After her session, she came to my classes to learn and gain insight as to how she could feel her daughter and connect with her angels to continue healing. Today, I am proud to call her my friend and she has inspired me with her journey and her everyday practice to healing.

The information and the messages I have shared throughout this healing guide and interactive workbook may resonate with you during different stages of your healing. I hope this offers you comfort during the difficult times. If you take anything away from this book, I hope it will be that love exists in both realms purely and freely. Love never extinguishes.

As it is said in the afterlife, "We do not say goodbye because we have not left you. Live each day knowing the joy and laughter is shared with us by your side. Till we meet again."

Thank you for your journey with me into afterlife and being open to the information. Feel free to share your photos and stories of your loved ones in a safe and healing environment on Instagram at #theothersideofaddiction or on my Facebook Group Page *The Other Side of Addiction*.

Treat yourself with love, compassion, and patience as each day is a new normal. Ask your loving angels and your loved ones crossed to walk with you each day. As you heal from the heaviness of grief and develop a trusted connection with the divine, build your inherent ability to feel, sense, and communicate with the other side.

With love,
Colleen

Angel Wisdom

Don't forget to follow:

www.ColleenStMichaels.com

Instagram: #OtherSideofAddiction

Facebook: The Other Side of Addiction- The Afterlife

Peace Warrior Deck

If you are looking for more guidance and help with messages on
your own, consider the *Peace Warrior Angel Card Deck*
by Colleen St. Michaels.

This beautiful deck was designed to help give you empowering
messages from your loved ones and angels to help encourage you.

In order to purchase, visit her website at
www.ColleenStMichaels.com/Shop/